P9-AFW-309

*A gift for:*_____

*From:*_____

God's Promises®

Day by Day

THOMAS NELSON

Since 1798

NASHVILLE   DALLAS   MEXICO CITY   RIO DE JANEIRO   BEIJING

Published in Nashvile, Tennessee by Thomas Nelson. Thomas Nelson is a trademark of Thomas Nelson, Inc.

Thomas Nelson, Inc. titles may be purchased in bulk for educational, business, fund-raising, or sales promotional use. For information, please e-mail SpecialMarkets@ThomasNelson.com

Unless otherwise indicated, all Scripture quotations in this book are from The New King James Version (NKJV) ©1979, 1980, 1982, 1992, Thomas Nelson, Inc., Publisher. Other Scripture references are from the following sources: The New American Standard Bible (NASB) © 1960, 1962, 1963, 1971, 1972, 1973, 1975, and 1977 by the Lockman Foundation. The New International Version of the Bible (NIV) © 1984 by the International Bible Society. Used by permission of Zondervan Bible Publishers. The Good News Bible: The Bible in Today's English Version (TEV) © 1976 by the American Bible Society. The New English Bible (NEB) © 1961, 1970, The Delegates of the Oxford University Press and The Syndics of the Cambridge University Press. The Message: The Bible in Contemporary Language (The Message) Copyright © 1993, 1994, 1995, 1996, 2000, 2001, 2002. Used by permission of NavPress Publishing Group. The New Century Version (NCV) ©1987, 1988, 1991 by W Publishing, Nashville, Tennessee. The Holy Bible, New Living Translation (NLT) © 1996. Used by permission of Tyndale House Publishers, Inc., Wheaton, Ill. All rights reserved.

Compiled and edited by Terri Gibbs

Designed by UDG | DesignWorks, Sisters, Oregon.

ISBN: 1-4041-0041-5 (Hardcover)
ISBN: 1-4041-0331-7 (Softcover)

www.thomasnelson.com

Printed and bound in China.

He who promised is faithful.

HEBREWS 10:23

January

The promises of God are dependable.

WARREN W. WIERSEBE

January 1

He who promised is faithful.

HEBREWS 10:23

A number of years ago, somebody counted the promises in the Bible and totaled up 7,474. I can't verify that number, but I do know that within the pages of the Bible there are thousands of promises that grab the reader and say, "Believe me! Accept me! Hold on to me!" And of all the promises in the Bible, the ones that often mean the most are the promises that offer hope at the end of affliction. Those promises that tell us, "It's worth it. Walk with Me. Trust Me. Wait with Me. I will reward you."

—CHARLES R. SWINDOLL
Joseph

His merciful kindness is great toward us.

PSALM 117:2

Kindness is invariably associated with mercy.
It is impossible to be kind without being
merciful. Likewise to be merciful is to be kind.
It implies that there is a deep and genuine concern
for another. This concern is one of compassion and
mercy. We are moved to be kind because we care.
Caring is the essence of God's selfless love
expressed to another.

—PHILLIP KELLER

A Gardner Looks at the Fruits of the Spirit

January 3

In Your hand is power and might; in Your hand it is to make great and to give strength to all.

1 CHRONICLES 29:12

The crowning jewel of Creation was man himself. He was created for a distinct purpose. If the purpose is lived out, life is fulfilling. If the purpose is rejected or ignored, life will never be what it was meant to be.

Apart from the Creator's purpose, you and I are like a light bulb lying in a meaningless, useless state. We need to fit into the Creator's original design, plugging into the power source—our relationship with Him—if our lives are to be what they were meant to be.

—ANNE GRAHAM LOTZ
God's Story

January 4

> *You cannot add any time
> to your life by worrying about it.*

MATTHEW 6:27, NCV

Anxiety is an expensive habit. Of course, it might be worth the cost if it worked. But it doesn't. Our frets are futile.

Worry has never brightened a day, solved a problem, or cured a disease.

God leads us. God will do the right thing at the right time. And what a difference that makes.

—MAX LUCADO
Traveling Light

January 5

*If the Son makes you free,
you shall be free indeed.*

JOHN 8:36

This freeing of the self is the real purpose of righteousness: the rightness that God asks of His children. Yet all too often we have thought that righteousness means the end of all our fun and freedom. Nothing could be further from the truth. God's love means sheer goodwill for us. Each of us can find the truth for ourselves only as we, step by step, walk the Faith Road, for God sees to it that sight never precedes faith.

—CATHERINE MARSHALL
Moments that Matter

January 6

*If any of you lacks wisdom, let him ask of
God, who gives to all liberally and
without reproach, and it will be given to him.*

JAMES 1:5

If you are smack-dab in the middle of a crisis
today, cry out to God. Tell Him exactly how you
feel. He can handle it. Someone once told me that
God is not embarrassed by the honesty of our
prayers. Get gut-level honest with God and tell
Him how badly you hurt, how angry you are, and
that you need His help to get through this crisis.
Don't worry about God—He can deal with this.

—JOHN HULL AND TIM ELMORE
Pivotal Praying

January 7

*The eyes of the LORD are on the righteous, and
His ears are open to their prayers.*

1 PETER 3:12

God knows what it is to need. The One who
caused water to burst from the rocks for the
Israelites had to ask a woman to bring Him a
simple drink from a well. The One robed in
splendor in the courts of heaven was stripped
naked and nailed to a cross. The One who created
the galaxies had to build fires to shield Himself
from the winter cold.

Meeting human need, then, is very much on
God's agenda. Human needs are not irrelevant or
unspiritual.

—MICHAEL YOUSSEF
The Prayer that God Answers

January 8

As He who called you is holy,
you also be holy in all your conduct.

1 PETER 1:15

No human is holy in himself. Holiness is foreign to us. It is alien. That is why we require the righteousness of Another to cover our moral nakedness. The Holy One has given us the holiness we need in the cloak of Christ's righteousness.

—R. C. SPROUL
In the Presence of God

January 9

*We can enter through a new and living way
that Jesus opened for us. It leads
through the curtain—Christ's body.*

HEBREWS 10:20, NCV

To the original readers, those last four words
were explosive: "the curtain—Christ's body."
According to the writer, the curtain equals Jesus.
Hence, whatever happened to the flesh of Jesus
happened to the curtain. What happened to His
flesh? It was torn. Torn by the whips, torn by the
thorns. Torn by the weight of the cross and the
point of the nails. But in the horror of His torn
flesh, we find the splendor of the open door. . . .

We are welcome to enter into God's presence—
any day, any time.

—MAX LUCADO
He Chose the Nails

LORD, who may abide in Your tabernacle?
He who walks uprightly, and works righteousness, and
speaks the truth in his heart.

PSALM 15:1–2

Y ou're invited to live with the Lord, to make
yourself at home with Him. But there's a
particular way to get there.

Walk uprightly. Work righteousness. Speak
the truth in your heart.

In short, let your life be cleansed and free and
full of all good things. Be saturated in His Spirit.

—PETER WALLACE
What the Psalmist Is Saying to You

January 11

I have loved you with an everlasting love; therefore
with lovingkindness I have drawn you.

JEREMIAH 31:3

We get in a hurry when we don't wait on the Lord. We jump ahead and do rash things. We shoot from the hip. We run off at the mouth, saying things that we later regret. But when we have sufficiently waited on the Lord, He gets full control of our spirit. At such moments, we're like a glove, and His hand is moving us wherever He pleases.

—CHARLES R. SWINDOLL
Esther

January 12

So you shall serve the LORD your God,
and He will bless your bread and your water.

EXODUS 23:25

Y ou may find temporary satisfaction in things
and people, but permanent, deep, full
satisfaction of your very being is only found in a
right relationship with God for Whom you were
created.

Not only is your *being* created for God, but
your *doing* is created for God also. You and I were
created for commitment to serve God.

—ANNE GRAHAM LOTZ
God's Story

January 13

*God is my strength and power, and
He makes my way perfect.*

2 SAMUEL 22:33

For the man or woman who recognizes the claim of Christ and gives allegiance to His absolute ownership, there comes the question of bearing His mark. The mark of the cross is what should identify us. The question is—does it?

Basically what it amounts to is this: A person exchanges the fickle fortunes of living life by sheer whimsy for the more productive and satisfying adventure of being guided by God.

—PHILLIP KELLER
A Shepherd Looks at Psalm 23

A faithful man will abound with blessings.

PROVERBS 28:20

Waiting is our destiny as creatures who cannot by themselves bring about what they hope for. We wait in the darkness for a flame we cannot light, we wait in fear for a happy ending we cannot write. We wait for a "not yet" that feels like a "not even." Waiting is the hardest work of hope.

—LEWIS SMEDES
Keeping Hope Alive

January 15

*To Him who is able to establish you . . . to God, alone
wise, be glory through Jesus Christ forever.*

ROMANS 16:25–27

God alone is the Source of all wisdom.
   A person may have natural logic. He or she
may have natural wisdom. But logic and wisdom err
in that they will always put the individual person
first. They are not supernatural wisdom.
   Supernatural wisdom comes only from God,
and it comes through Jesus Christ—the
personification of God's wisdom to us.

—LARRY LEA
Wisdom: The Gift Worth Seeking

But You, O LORD, are a God full of compassion,
and gracious, longsuffering
and abundant in mercy and truth.

PSALM 86:15

L ike the father in the parable about the Prodigal
Son, God is waiting, looking, His eyes glued to
the horizon searching for us. When He sees us,
though He is a dignified patriarch, He lifts up His
garment and shamelessly gallops toward us, as we
come trudging toward Him with our load of guilt
and despair. He wraps us in His arms and
smothers us with kisses.

This is not new behavior for God. He has
looked at people with compassion for centuries.

—PAUL E. MILLER
Love Walked Among Us

It is to your advantage that I go away;
for if I do not go away, the Helper will not come to you;
but if I depart, I will send Him to you.

JOHN 16:7

When Jesus left this world He went to the Father. His ascension was to a certain place for a particular reason. To ascend did not mean merely "to go up." He was being elevated to the right hand of the Father. The seat He occupies on His departure is the royal throne of cosmic authority. It is the office of the King of the Kings and the Lord of the Lords.

—R. C. SPROUL
In the Presence of God

January 18

I will turn their mourning to joy,
will comfort them, and
make them rejoice rather than sorrow.

JEREMIAH 31:13

Human beings by nature want to hug life and hold onto it, choke it down, save it and keep it. But Jesus taught there's only one way to know life's meaning: We gain happiness by letting go of this life.

What is joy? It is Christ.

—CALVIN MILLER
Into the Depths of God

January 19

If you keep My commandments,
you will abide in my love.

JOHN 15:10

Learning to pray is learning to trust the wisdom, the power, and the love of our Heavenly Father, always so far beyond our dreams. He knows our need and knows ways to meet it that have never entered our heads. Things we feel sure we need for happiness may often lead to our ruin. Things we think will ruin us, . . . if we believe what the Father tells us and surrender ourselves into His strong arms, bring us deliverance and joy.

—ELISABETH ELLIOT
Keep a Quiet Heart

January 20

It is no longer I who live,
but it is Christ who lives in me.

GALATIANS 2:19

Little by little we are changed by this daily
crucifixion of the will. Changed, not like a
tornado changes things, but like a grain of sand in
an oyster changes things. New graces emerge: new
ability to cast all our care upon God, new joy at the
success of others, new hope in a God who is good. . . .

God is not destroying the will but
transforming it so that over a process of time and
experience we can freely will what God wills.

—RICHARD FOSTER
Prayer: Finding the Heart's True Home

January 21

*You have filled my heart with
greater joy than when their grain
and new wine abound.*

PSALM 4:7, NIV

In David's time, the hope of many rested upon
the outcome of the year's harvest. If the crops
were plentiful, the community rejoiced. If the
crops failed, the community despaired.

But David experienced a joy that flourished
even when crops perished. He treasured a joy that
thrived even through drought. David knew a joy
that was pure. Such joy flows from one source: the
living God.

—ALICIA BRITT CHOLE
Pure Joy

January 22

Let them shout for joy and be glad,
who favor my righteous cause.

PSALM 35:27

God is a deeply, profoundly passionate person. Zeal consumes Him. It is the secret of His life, the writer of Hebrews says. The "joy set before him" enabled Jesus to endure the agony of the Cross (Heb. 12:2, NIV). In other words, His profound desire for something greater sustained Him at the moment of His deepest trial.

—JOHN ELDREDGE
The Journey of Desire

January 23

Do not grieve the Holy Spirit of God, by whom you were sealed for the day of redemption.

EPHESIANS 4:30

If you are like I am, you love surprises.

The greatest surprise you will ever experience is the surprising joy that comes when God, through His Holy Spirit, fills your heart to the fullest. Your days will be filled with more than you would ever ask or even dream of.

—NEIL CLARK WARREN
God Said It, Don't Sweat It

January 24

*Let all those rejoice who put their trust
in You; let them ever shout
for joy, because You defend them.*

PSALM 5:11

God told us from the very beginning that in love—His love—we find the answer to all our needs as well as healing for our broken souls.

When your heart is anchored to the heart of Jesus Christ, you will find Him near and always eager to confirm His personal love for you. The love of the world will pass away, but God's love is guaranteed never to fade. He is the Source of all true, lasting love.

—CHARLES STANLEY
Into His Presence

January 25

*You have been born again, not
of perishable seed, but of imperishable, through the
living and enduring word of God.*

1 PETER 1:23, NIV

The only way to get into the human family is to be born. Everybody you meet has a birthday every year because birth is the method God has ordained for transmitting human life from one generation to the next.

What's true of the physical is also true of the spiritual: the only way to possess God's life and enter God's family is through birth.

—WARREN W. WIERSEBE
The Twenty Essential Qualities

January 26

*Pray without ceasing. . . . He who
calls you is faithful, who also will do it.*

1 THESSALONIANS 5:17, 24

Jesus taught that answered prayer requires persistence. There may be a period when the door of blessing on which we hammer in prayer remains shut to us. Yet if we persist in knocking, the promise is that God will eventually open the door.

—CATHERINE MARSHALL
Moments that Matter

January 27

*Your testimonies are wonderful; therefore
my soul keeps them.*

PSALM 119:129

There are those who regard the Bible principally as the history of Israel. Others admit that it sets forth the soundest ethics ever enunciated. But these things, important as they are, are only incidental to the real theme of the Bible, which is the story of God's redemption as it exists in Jesus Christ.

Those who read the Scriptures as magnificent literature, breath-taking poetry or history, and overlook the story of Salvation, miss the Bible's real meaning and message.

—BILLY GRAHAM
Peace with God

January 28

> *[They] nailed him to a cross. . . . This*
> *was God's plan which he had made long ago.*

ACTS 2:23, NCV

Jesus' death was not the result of a panicking cosmological engineer. The cross wasn't a tragic surprise. Calvary was not a knee-jerk response to a world plummeting toward destruction. It wasn't a patch-up job or a stop-gap measure. . . .

The moment the forbidden fruit touched the lips of Eve, the shadow of a cross appeared on the horizon. And between that moment and the moment the man with the mallet placed the spike against the wrist of God, a master plan was fulfilled.

—MAX LUCADO
God Came Near

January 29

Since He Himself was tempted, . . . He is
able to come to the aid of those who are tempted.

HEBREWS 2:18, NASB

Having been swamped by sin all our lives, struggling to find our way to the top of the water to breathe, we can find great hope in the ability God gives us not only to breathe but to swim freely. You see, Christ not only lived an exemplary life, He also makes it possible for us to do the same. He gives us His pattern to follow *without* while at the same time providing the needed power *within.*

—CHARLES R. SWINDOLL
Joseph

January 30

I stand at the door and knock.
If anyone hears My voice and opens the
door, I will come in to him.

REVELATION 3:20

God's invitation is clear and nonnegotiable.... Isn't it incredible that God leaves the choice to us?

Think about it. There are many things in life we can't choose. We can't, for example, choose the weather. We can't control the economy. We can't choose whether or not we are born with a big nose or blue eyes or a lot of hair.... But we can choose where we spend eternity. The big choice, God leaves to us.

—MAX LUCADO
And the Angels Were Silent

January 31

In all their distress, he too was distressed; . . .
he lifted them up and carried them.

ISAIAH 63:9, NIV

The solution to loneliness is not to give in or give up or do what everyone else does or go where everyone else goes or look like and speak like and think like and act like the world around you so you won't stand out so sharply from the crowd. The solution is not to withdraw into an uninvolved, inactive life. The solution is found when we discover meaning in the midst of loneliness as God Himself shares our loneliness while we walk with and work for Him.

—ANNE GRAHAM LOTZ
God's Story

February

Our faith is not based on
speculation but upon God and His word.

BILLY GRAHAM

February 1

*You will show me the path of life; in Your
presence is fullness of joy; at Your right hand
are pleasures forevermore.*

PSALM 16:11

Christ was the most balanced and perhaps the
most beloved being ever to enter the society of
men. Not only was He gentle and tender and true
but also righteous, stern as steel, and terribly
tough on phony people.

He was magnificent in His magnanimous spirit
of forgiveness for fallen folk but a terror to those
who indulged in double talk or false pretenses.

He came to set men free from their own sins,
their own selves, their own fears. Those so liberated
loved Him with fierce loyalty.

—PHILLIP KELLER
A Shepherd Looks at Psalm 23

February 2

*Faith comes by hearing,
and hearing by the word of God.*

ROMANS 10:17

Why would Bible reading produce faith?
Certainly not because there is something
magical about the book. The real reasons are far
more direct . . . : (1) We can scarcely claim God's
promises for ourselves until we know what He has
promised. (2) The Bible is a series of true stories of
God's dealing with men and women quite like us.

There are pioneers, adventurers, and
businessmen. . . . When we read this book
intelligently, we learn how God deals with
humankind, what He is like, and what we can
expect from Him.

—CATHERINE MARSHALL
Moments that Matter

February 3

Casting all your care upon Him,
for He cares for you.

1 PETER 5:7

To know God, or even to begin to know Him, is
to know that we are not alone in the universe.
Someone Else is Out There. There is a hint that
there may be a refuge for our loneliness. To stop
our frantic getting, spending, and searching, and
simply to *look* at the things God has made is to
move one step away from despair, for God cares.
The most awesome seascape can reveal a care that
is actually *tender.*

—ELISABETH ELLIOT
The Path of Loneliness

February 4

*It is God who works in you both
to will and to do for His good pleasure.*

PHILIPPIANS 2:13

The only purpose or intention God ever has is altogether good. When the Bible speaks of the sovereign exercise of the pleasure of His will, there is no hint of arbitrariness or wicked intent. The pleasure of His will is always the good pleasure of His will. His pleasure is always good; His will is always good; His intentions are always good.

—R. C. SPROUL
In the Presence of God

February 5

He himself is our peace ... and has destroyed the barrier, the dividing wall of hostility.

EPHESIANS 2:14, NIV

We are guilty and He is innocent.
We are filthy and He is pure.
We are wrong and He is right.
He is not on that cross for His sins. He is there for ours.

—MAX LUCADO
Six Hours One Friday

February 6

*The LORD is my rock and my fortress
and my deliverer; my God,
my strength, in whom I will trust.*

PSALM 18:2

God is strong. Solid as a rock. Protective as a fortress and a shield. He is your place of shelter.

His strength is perfect and complete. It's a resource that cannot be exhausted. And it's available to you. So whenever you feel absolutely weak and defeated, vulnerable to sin or depression or failure, draw on His strength. Run to Him.

—PETER WALLACE
What the Psalmist Is Saying to You

February 7

*I will heal them and reveal
to them the abundance of peace and truth.*

JEREMIAH 33:6

God caused the Bible to be written for the express purpose of revealing to man God's plan for redemption. God caused this Book to be written that He might make His everlasting laws clear to His children, and that they might have His great wisdom to guide them and His great love to comfort them as they make their way through life. For without the Bible, this world would indeed be a dark and frightening place, without signpost or beacon.

— BILLY GRAHAM
Peace with God

February 8

*Humble yourselves in the
presence of the Lord, and He will exalt you.*

JAMES 4:10, NASB

God can use our authority and our abundance
and our promotion. But before He can, we
need to humble ourselves before God's mighty
hand and say, "Jesus Christ, I need You. I have all
of this to account for, and I can't take any of it
with me. Please use me as you see fit." With
authority comes the need for accountability.
With popularity comes the need for humility. With
prosperity comes the need for integrity.

—CHARLES R. SWINDOLL
Joseph

February 9

*The hope of the righteous
will be gladness.*

PROVERBS 10:28

One of the great themes of Christianity is triumphant hope. Not just hope as in a distant, vague dream, but *triumphant* hope, the kind of hope where all things end right. In the midst of the struggles and the storms and the sufferings of life, we can advance our thoughts beyond today and see relief . . . triumph . . . victory. Because, in the end, God does indeed win.

—CHARLES R. SWINDOLL
Esther

*I did not come to judge the world
but to save the world.*

JOHN 12:47

We'll often notice things wrong with people, but does that initial look lead to compassion and helping, or to judging and distance? Compassion and judging are two different ways of "seeing."

When we stop judging, we rest from the incessant work of analyzing others. We don't need to figure out what's wrong with people—that's God's job. Our job is to try to understand.

—PAUL E. MILLER
Love Walked Among Us

The LORD is good; His mercy is everlasting, and
His truth endures to all generations.

PSALM 100:5

Truth is timeless. Truth does not differ from one age to another, from one people to another, from one geographical location to another. Men's ideas may differ, men's customs may change, men's moral codes may vary, but God's great all-prevailing Truth stands for time and eternity.

—BILLY GRAHAM
Peace with God

February 12

The LORD is their strength, and
He is the saving refuge of His anointed.

PSALM 28:8

O nce we give ourselves up to God, shall we attempt to get hold of what can never belong to us—*tomorrow?* Our lives are His, our times in His hand. He is Lord over what will happen, never mind what may happen. When we prayed "Thy will be done," did we suppose He did not hear us? He heard indeed, and daily makes our business His. If my life is once surrendered, all is well. Let me not grab it back, as though it were in peril in His hand but would be safer in mine!

—ELISABETH ELLIOT
Keep a Quiet Heart

February 13

*The LORD gives wisdom; from His mouth come
knowledge and understanding.*

PROVERBS 2:6

God alone is wise. He makes His wisdom
available to you, but you must first want
it . . . feel a need of it . . . yes, REQUIRE, it as
essential in your life. Then, and only then, are you
putting yourself in a position to partake of God's
wisdom and become wise.

—LARRY LEA
Wisdom: The Gift Worth Seeking

*Whatever God does, it
shall be forever.*

ECCLESIASTES 3:14

Though God's people often forgot their God, God
didn't forget them. He kept His word. The land
became theirs.

When Joseph was dropped into a pit by his
own brothers, God didn't give up.

When Moses said, "Here I am, send Aaron,"
God didn't give up. . . .

When Peter worshiped Him at the supper and
cursed Him at the fire, He didn't give up.

God never gives up.

—MAX LUCADO
Six Hours One Friday

February 15

He who has begun a good work in you
will complete it until the day of Jesus Christ.

PHILIPPIANS 1:6

God is looking for those who believe that what He says is more important than what anyone else says. That what He thinks is more important than what anyone else thinks. That what He wants is more important than what anyone else wants. That His will is more important than their own.

God is looking for another Noah. Another Meshach. Another Shadrach. Another Abednego.

One person with God is not alone but a majority!

—ANNE GRAHAM LOTZ
God's Story

February 16

*God will wipe away every tear
from their eyes; there shall be no more death,
nor sorrow, nor crying.*

REVELATION 21:4

Christians celebrate the death of Jesus in the Lord's Supper to remember that He died on the cross for the sins of the world. But the supper does not end with the recollection of suffering. We listen to the Lord telling His disciples to repeat this same memorial until He returns. Listening, we rekindle our hope that He will indeed return and that, when He does, God will make His world work right again for everyone.

—LEWIS SMEDES
Keeping Hope Alive

February 17

God is greater than our heart,
and knows all things.

1 JOHN 3:20

You and I are governed. The weather determines what we wear. The terrain tells us how to travel. Gravity dictates our speed, and health determines our strength. We may challenge these forces and alter them slightly, but we never remove them.

God—our Shepherd—doesn't check the weather; He makes it. He doesn't defy gravity; He created it.

God is what He is. What He has always been. God is Yahweh—an unchanging God, an uncaused God, and an ungoverned God.

—MAX LUCADO
Traveling Light

February 18

Teach us to number our days,
that we may gain a heart of wisdom.

PSALM 90:12

In very truth I have only today. Yesterday is gone forever. There is no guarantee I shall be here tomorrow. So in reality I am locked into a single *day-tight* time and space concept. I have the choice—either I can worry my way through it or I can revel and rejoice in this interval of time provided by my Father.

—PHILLIP KELLER
A Gardner Looks at the Fruits of the Spirit

February 19

*You are my lamp, O LORD; the LORD
shall enlighten my darkness.*

2 SAMUEL 22:29

Knowledge of the Bible is essential to a rich and meaningful life, for the words of this Book have a way of filling in the missing pieces, of bridging the gaps, of turning the tarnished colors of our life to jewel-like brilliance. Learn to take your every problem to the Bible. Within its pages you will find the correct answer.

— BILLY GRAHAM
Peace with God

February 20

*You are My friends if
you do whatever I command you.*

JOHN 15:14

There are no miseries in heaven. There is no
hardship or pain in heaven. Only contentment,
and joy, and perfect peace. When you enjoy doing
the will of God, you are bringing heaven into
your heart. Do you want a piece of heaven on
earth? Obey the will of God.

—MICHAEL YOUSSEF
The Prayer That God Answers

February 21

I have come that they may have life,
and that they may have it more abundantly.

JOHN 10:10

In the cross, the Lord God arranged a plan for
our spiritual survival with divine integrity.
It required the sacrifice of Christ on the cross.
He followed through. We can take Him at His
word. He was who He said He was, and He did
what He said He would do. With a single heart
and a single mind and a single will, He fulfilled
the Father's plan.

—CHARLES R. SWINDOLL
Joseph

February 22

*He who heeds the word wisely will find good, and
whoever trusts in the LORD, happy is he.*

PROVERBS 16:20

When you find yourself drowning in
overwhelming circumstances, ask God to
give you a promise to which you can cling—
a promise on which you can base your hope. Hope
that is based simply on what you want or what you
feel is not a genuine expression of faith.

Our hope must be based on God's word.

—ANNE GRAHAM LOTZ
God's Story

He makes me to lie down in green pastures;
He leads me beside the still waters.

PSALM 23:2

Note the two pronouns preceding the two verbs.
He makes me . . . He leads me. . . .
Who is in charge? The shepherd. The shepherd
selects the trail and prepares the pasture. The
sheep's job—our job—is to watch the shepherd.

—MAX LUCADO
Traveling Light

February 24

He will be very gracious to you
at the sound of your cry; when He hears it,
He will answer you.

ISAIAH 30:19

Be specific in your prayer life. If you need a job, pray for a job. If you're an engineer, ask God to open up an engineering position for you, or something related for which you are qualified.... If you need fifteen hundred dollars for tuition, ask for that amount. Make your petitions specific.

—CHARLES R. SWINDOLL
Elijah

February 25

I will wait for the God of my salvation;
my God will hear me.

MICAH 7:7

Even in the Garden of Gethsemane on the night of betrayal, Christ had plenty of time and opportunity to flee.

But He would not flee. Instead He knelt to pray in the shadowy Garden under the gray-green leaves of the olive tress. And in His prayer that night, Jesus gave us, for all time, the perfect pattern for the Prayer of Relinquishment: "Not what I want, but what You want." . . . Jesus deliberately set Himself to make His will and God's will the same.

—CATHERINE MARSHALL
Moments that Matter

*Your thoughts toward us cannot be
recounted to You in order; if I would declare
and speak of them, they are
more than can be numbered.*

PSALM 40:5

As a watch must have a designer, so our precision-like universe has a Great Designer. We call Him God. His is a name with which we are familiar. From earliest childhood we have breathed His name. The Bible declares that the God we talk about, the God we sing about, the God "from whom all blessing flow!" is the God who created this world and placed us in it.

— BILLY GRAHAM
Peace with God

*Behold, God is my salvation, I will
trust and not be afraid.*

ISAIAH 12:2

God deals with the hard questions of life.
Not questions like how do I make a living,
but how do I make a life? Not how do I spend my
time, but how do I spend eternity? And not so
much how do I get along with the person who sits
next to me, but ultimately, how do I get along with
God? When we answer the hard questions
correctly, all the others fall into place.

—CHARLES R. SWINDOLL
Joseph

February 28

[He] is able to do exceedingly abundantly
above all that we ask or think.

EPHESIANS 3:20

Instead of raging against the Lord for the way
He manages our lives, let us carefully consider
all the benefits He bestows. Take a piece of paper;
sit down alone in a quiet spot; write down one by
one all the good things—the delights and the
pleasures He has made possible for you. List
everything—the sound of music; the laughter of
children; the sunrise; the scent of a rose; the clasp
of a friend's hand; the loyalty of a dog. If one is
honest, there is no end to the list.

—PHILLIP KELLER
A Gardner Looks at the Fruits of the Spirit

March

A strong faith leads to a good attitude.

CHARLES R. SWINDOLL

March 1

Godliness with contentment is great gain.

1 TIMOTHY 6:6

When we surrender to God the cumbersome sack of discontent, we don't just give up something; we gain something. God replaces it with a lightweight, tailor-made, sorrow-resistant attaché of gratitude.

What will you gain with contentment? You may gain your marriage. You may gain precious hours with your children. You may gain your self-respect. You may gain joy.

—MAX LUCADO
Traveling Light

You are a chosen generation,
a royal priesthood, . . . the people of God.

1 PETER 2:9–10

Several images are used in the Bible to describe
the Church: the Body of Christ, the elect,
the house of God, the saints. One of the most
meaningful expressions the Bible uses is "the
people of God," the *laos theon.*

The Church is not a building; it is not the
clergy; it is not an abstract institution—it is the
people of God.

—R. C. SPROUL
In the Presence of God

March 3

It is God who arms me with strength,
and makes my way perfect.

PSALM 18:32

Who is God? He is the Lord. He is the Sovereign Ruler of the universe. He is intimately involved in your life. He knows what you're feeling and why. He knows what you need, and He will give it as you can receive it.

He is a rock—strong, bold, mighty, immovable, unyielding in power.

The Lord your God will guide you right.

—PETER WALLACE
What the Psalmist Is Saying to You

March 4

Take my yoke upon you and learn from Me . . .
and you will find rest for your souls.

MATTHEW 11:29

Discipleship is the call to Calvary, first and foremost to receive the forgiveness and salvation provided by God's great love. But we are never to remain solely as forgiven penitents. We are called to grow as God's sons and daughters, to serve as His faithful stewards, to learn as His devoted disciples. And all of that growth, service, and learning is most practically processed not by the way we handle life's blessings, but by the way we live through its bad days.

—JACK HAYFORD
How to Live Through a Bad Day

*Every word of God is pure; He is
a shield to those who put their trust in Him.*

PROVERBS 30:5

God has not changed. If He was faithful to watch over Noah and all those within the ark, bringing them safely through the storm, He will do the same for you. Just as He was faithful to preserve Joseph through thirteen years of slavery in Potiphar's house and Pharaoh's prison, just as He was faithful to preserve the little baby Moses floating on the Nile . . . *God will be faithful to you.*

—ANNE GRAHAM LOTZ
God's Story

March 6

Blessed are those who keep justice,
and he who does righteousness at all times!

PSALM 106:3

We rejoice over each day we can live for God. We give hearty and humble thanks for His abundant and gracious care, living in a constant "attitude of gratitude." To live this way is to live out in the open sunlight of His presence. It is to live in honest dignity and strength and serene simplicity. It is to live above the clutter and complications of a complex society that would crowd and choke out our fruitfulness for God.

—PHILLIP KELLER
A Gardner Looks at the Fruits of the Spirit

> *GOD's business is putting things
> right; he loves getting the lines straight.*
>
> PSALM 11:7, THE MESSAGE

In the wilderness of loneliness we are terribly vulnerable. What we want is OUT, and sometimes there appear to be some easy ways to get there. Will we take Satan up on his offers, satisfy our desires in ways never designed by God, seek security outside of His holy will? If we do, we may find a measure of happiness, but not the lasting joy our heavenly Father wants us to have.

—ELISABETH ELLIOT
The Path of Loneliness

*Walk in love, as Christ also has
loved us and given Himself for us.*

EPHESIANS 5:2

D o you love others? Do you love others as you
love yourself? If so, you are undoubtedly in a
right relationship with God! But if you find
yourself focusing all of your attention on your
own life exclusive of others, you can know for a
fact that you haven't loved yourself the way you
need to. All the love you need is totally available
to you right now! God is ready to love you so
powerfully that your love for others will become
automatic and natural.

—NEIL CLARK WARREN
God Said It, Don't Sweat It

March 9

*This is the victory that has
overcome the world—our faith.*

1 JOHN 5:4

There is a difference between acceptance and
resignation.

Resignation is barren of faith in the love of
God. It says, "Grievous circumstances have come
to me. There is no escaping them."

Acceptance says, "I trust the goodwill, the
love of my God. I'll open my arms and my
understanding to what He has allowed to come
to me." Thus acceptance leaves the door of hope
wide open to God's creative plan.

—CATHERINE MARSHALL
Moments that Matter

March 10

[God] is right in everything he does.

DANIEL 9:14, NCV

God is never wrong. He has never rendered a wrong decision, experienced the wrong attitude, taken the wrong path, said the wrong thing, or acted the wrong way. He is never too late or too early, too loud or too soft, too fast or too slow. He has always been and always will be right. He is righteous.

—MAX LUCADO
Traveling Light

*He who believes in the Son of God
has the witness in himself.*

1 JOHN 5:10

Man's only salvation from sin stands on a lonely, barren, skull-shaped hill; a thief hangs on one cross, a murderer on another, and between them, a Man with a crown of thorns. Blood flows from His hands and feet, it pours from His side, it drops down His face—while those who stand looking on sneer and mock.

Who is this tortured figure, this Man whom other men seek to humiliate and kill? He is the Son of God, the Prince of Peace.

—BILLY GRAHAM
Peace with God

March 12

The fear of the LORD is
the beginning of wisdom.

PSALM 111:10

Persons who fear the Lord are persons who can hardly wait to do the commandments of God. They are a delight, not a chore. They are exciting, not boring. They are thrilling, not devastating. When God says something to persons who fear the Lord, they are EAGER to jump into action and get the job done! They have a sense of holy excitement.

—LARRY LEA
Wisdom: The Gift Worth Seeking

March 13

Be kind to one another, . . . forgiving one another.

EPHESIANS 4:32

Forgiving is a minor miracle, a bloodless surgery we perform on our spirits. It goes like this, though not necessarily in this order: (1) We begin to see the offender as a . . . blemished person not all that much different from ourselves. (2) We surrender our precious right to get even . . . and choose to live with the scales unbalanced. (3) We gradually, oh so gradually, find the will to wish him well.

Once begun—and remember that it is almost always a process, sometimes a lifelong journey— we . . . have hope again. People who discover the grace to forgive almost always discover the grace of hope besides.

—LEWIS SMEDES
Keeping Hope Alive

*Christ died for sins once for all, the righteous for the
unrighteous, to bring you to God.*

1 PETER 3:18, NIV

The path of righteousness is a narrow, winding
trail up a steep hill. At the top of the hill is a
cross. At the base of the cross are bags. Countless
bags full of innumerable sins. Calvary is the
compost pile of guilt. Would you like to leave
yours there as well?

—MAX LUCADO
Traveling Light

*The wages of sin is death, but the gift of God is eternal
life in Christ Jesus our Lord.*

ROMANS 6:23

The cross, sin's masterpiece of shame and hate,
became God's masterpiece of mercy and
forgiveness. Through the death of Christ upon the
cross, sin itself was crucified for those who believe
in Him. Sin was conquered on the cross. His death
is the foundation of our hope, the promise of our
triumph!

— BILLY GRAHAM
Peace with God

March 16

Blessed is that man
who makes the LORD his trust.

PSALM 40:4

When the Israelites left Egypt, they headed across the Red Sea to Mount Sinai. From there it was only about a two-week journey into the promised land. Fourteen days turned into *forty years*. A blind camel would have found its way sooner than that. God designed a supernaturally long trail in order to deal with what was in their hearts.

—JOHN ELDREDGE
The Journey of Desire

March 17

The heavens are Yours, the earth also is Yours; . . .
You have a mighty arm; strong is Your hand.

PSALM 89:11, 13

As you and I see the winter snows give way to
spring flowers and the summer's heat give way
to autumn's briskness, we are reminded that in back
of the changes is the God Who never changes.
The sun that always rises every morning and
always sets every evening, the stars that always
come out in the night sky, and the moon that
always goes through its monthly phases—all reveal
the glory of God, Who is good!

—ANNE GRAHAM LOTZ
God's Story

March 18

Trust God from the bottom of your heart;
don't try to figure out everything on your own.

PROVERBS 3:5, *THE MESSAGE*

Whatever life gives us opportunity to do, let us do it well. Let us do it to the best of our ability, then leave the results with Christ.

It is not for us to decide or determine what the net results of our living will be. It is God who keeps the eternal accounts. Only He can ascertain what is of consequence in His economy.

—PHILLIP KELLER
A Gardner Looks at the Fruits of the Spirit

March 19

There is no fear in love;
but perfect love casts out fear.

1 JOHN 4:18

The unconditional love we so desperately need if we are to become authentic comes only from God. Interestingly enough, it is when we let God love us unconditionally at a deep level that we tend to become the person He really wants us to be. It is only when we feel His total love for us that we are free to be genuine in all of our relations with others. This genuineness, I feel confident, is exactly what pleases Him most.

—NEIL CLARK WARREN
God Said It, Don't Sweat It

March 20

*In quietness and confidence
shall be your strength.*

ISAIAH 30:15

God never forgets anything He promises.
That's right . . . never.

God's agenda continues to unfold right on
schedule, even when there is not a shred of evidence
that He remembers. Even when the most extreme
events transpire and "life just doesn't seem fair,"
God is there, carrying out His providential plan
exactly as He pre-arranged it. He keeps His word.

—CHARLES R. SWINDOLL
Elijah

March 21

*A man has joy by the answer of his mouth,
and a word spoken in due season, how good it is!*

PROVERBS 15:23

Mark Twain once said that the difference between the right word and the nearly right word is the difference between lightning and a lightning bug. In other words, it's huge. What we say and don't say . . . matters.

Words have the power to heal and to hurt. They have the ability to win people over or wound them for years to come. It's very important that we choose our words wisely. . . . God can help us with that if we ask Him.

—JOHN HULL AND TIM ELMORE
Pivotal Praying

March 22

*The fear of the LORD
is the instruction of wisdom.*

PROVERBS 15:33

Freedom to choose or to reject, freedom to obey
God's commands or to go contrary to them,
freedom to make himself happy or miserable. For it
is not the mere possession of freedom that makes
life satisfying—it is what we choose to do with our
freedom that determines whether or not we shall
find peace with God and with ourselves.

—BILLY GRAHAM
Peace with God

March 23

*The cross of our Lord Jesus Christ is
my only reason for bragging.*

GALATIANS 6:14, NCV

Do you feel a need for affirmation? Does your
self-esteem need attention? You don't need to
drop names or show off. You need only pause at
the base of the cross and be reminded of this: The
maker of the stars would rather die for you than
live without you. And that is a fact. So if you need
to brag, brag about that.

—MAX LUCADO
Traveling Light

March 24

*Hope does not disappoint, because the love
of God has been poured out in our hearts by the Holy
Spirit who was given to us.*

ROMANS 5:5

Have you become so overwhelmed with your own weakness and failure and sin and inability to live a life that is pleasing to God that you have begun to doubt your salvation? Then look up! Take a good, long look at the cross and remember that God *remembers.* He loves you, He has forgiven you, He is eternally committed to you, and you are saved! Forever! Praise God! His covenant is unconditional!

—ANNE GRAHAM LOTZ
God's Story

March 25

Fear not, for I am with you.

ISAIAH 41:10

God knows where we are. Sometimes we forget this. Sometimes we even feel that God has forgotten us. He hasn't. God knows exactly where we are. So when you are afflicted with those forsaken feelings, when you're on the verge of throwing a pity party, thanks to those despairing thoughts, go back to the Word of God. God says, "I know where you are."

—CHARLES R. SWINDOLL
Elijah

March 26

Because he has set his love upon Me,
therefore I will deliver him; I will set him on high,
because he has known My name.

PSALM 91:14

The first step toward God is realizing you are on the wrong path going the wrong way. It's actually quite freeing if you think about it. With your mask off you can get real and relax.

When we realize we don't have it all together, we can care for people because we no longer feel morally superior to them. Consequently, we are quicker to help than to give advice, quicker to listen than to lecture.

—PAUL E. MILLER
Love Walked Among Us

He will rejoice over you with gladness,
He will quiet you with His love.

ZEPHANIAH 3:17

What happens when we find ourselves in the kingdom of God? The disabled jump to their feet and start doing a jig. The deaf go out and buy themselves stereo equipment. The blind are headed to the movies. The dead are not dead at all anymore, but very much alive. They show up for dinner. In other words, human brokenness in all its forms is healed. The kingdom of God brings *restoration.*

—JOHN ELDREDGE
The Journey of Desire

*As the heavens are higher than the earth,
so are My ways higher than your ways, and My
thoughts than your thoughts.*

ISAIAH 55:9

When we begin praying for others, we soon discover that it is easy to become discouraged at the results, which seem frustratingly slow and uneven. This is because we are entering the strange mix of divine influence and human autonomy. God never compels. . . .

His way is like the rain and the snow that gently fall to the earth, disappearing into the ground as they nourish it. When the time is right, up springs new life. No manipulation, no control; perfect freedom, perfect liberty.

—RICHARD FOSTER
Prayer: Finding the Heart's True Home

March 29

He leads me in the paths of righteousness
for His name's sake.

PSALM 23:3

What the shepherd does with the flock, our Shepherd will do with us. He will lead us to the high country. When the pasture is bare down here. God will lead us up there. He will guide us through the gate, out of the flatlands, and up the path of the mountain.

—MAX LUCADO
Traveling Light

He knows the way I take; when He has tried me,
I shall come forth as gold.

JOB 23:10, NASB

The key phrase in that statement is "when He has tried me." You see, there is no hurry-up process for finding and shaping gold. The process of discovering, processing, purifying, and shaping gold is a lengthy, painstaking process. Affliction is gold in the making for the child of God, and God is the one who determines how long the process takes. He alone is the Refiner.

—CHARLES R. SWINDOLL
Joseph

March 31

I am going there to prepare a place for you.
After I go and prepare a place for you, I will come back
and take you to be with me.

JOHN 14:2-3, NCV

Note the promise of Jesus. "I will come back and take you to be with me." Jesus pledges to take us home. He does not delegate this task. He may send missionaries to teach you, angels to protect you, teachers to guide you, singers to inspire you, and physicians to heal you, but He sends no one to take you. He reserves this job for Himself.

—MAX LUCADO
Traveling Light

April

❧

God's promises are true forever.

CHARLES STANLEY

April 1

God is love.

1 JOHN 4:8

Never question God's great love, for it is as unchangeable a part of God as is His holiness. No matter how terrible your sins, God loves you. Were it not for the love of God, none of us would ever have a chance in the future life. But God is Love! And His love for us is everlasting!

— BILLY GRAHAM
Peace with God

April 2

He will teach us His ways,
and we shall walk in His paths.

MICAH 4:2

When we ask God to guide us, we have to accept by faith that He is doing so. This means that when He closes a door in our faces, we do well not to try to crash that door.

The promise is that the Shepherd will go ahead of the sheep; His method is to clear the way for us.

—CATHERINE MARSHALL
Moments that Matter

April 3

Good and upright is the LORD;
therefore He teaches sinners in the way.

PSALM 25:8

Shame is a deep, dark wound that scars our
hearts. When we feel shame, we are vulnerable
to attacks and then to deeper shame.

Rather than get caught in shame's downward
spiral, we can stop the process by lifting our
damaged hearts up to the Lord. We can look to
Him for release from the past hurts and relief
from the present troubles. Look to the One you
can trust for mercy and acceptance.

—PETER WALLACE
What the Psalmist Is Saying to You

April 4

*If you have faith as a mustard seed,
you will say to this mountain "Move from here
to there," and it will move.*

MATTHEW 17:20

Don't measure the size of the mountain; talk to
the One who can move it. Instead of carrying
the world on your shoulders, talk to the One who
holds the universe on His. Hope is a look away.

—MAX LUCADO
Traveling Light

April 5

Jesus Christ came into the world to save sinners.

1 TIMOTHY 1:15

God designed and created you because He loves you.... But you drifted in the currents of sin and were swept from Him into the world. He worked for years, making the necessary arrangements to buy you back. Finally everything was ready. The purchase price He counted out was not nickels and dimes and quarters, it was the blood of His own dear Son. As He strode victoriously out of the tomb on Easter morning, you could almost feel Him hugging you to Himself, whispering triumphantly, "You're twice mine! I made you at Creation; now I've bought you at Calvary!"

—ANNE GRAHAM LOTZ
God's Story

April 6

*The LORD longs to be gracious
to you, and therefore He waits on high to
have compassion on you.*

ISAIAH 30:18, NASB

D o you long for God? I've got great news! In an
even greater way—greater than you could
ever imagine—He longs to be gracious to you.
He is offering you all the things you hunger for.
The table is loaded, and He is smiling, waiting
for you to sit down and enjoy the feast He
prepared with you in mind. Have a seat—grace
is being served.

—CHARLES R. SWINDOLL
Joseph

I love those who love me, and
those who seek me diligently will find me.

PROVERBS 8:17

The love of God is the very life of God.

That life, if allowed to grow freely in the good ground of the well-prepared soil of our souls, will flourish.

Such fruit can and does come only from above. It is not something we can counterfeit. The very life of God, epitomized in the love of God, originates only and always with Him.

—PHILLIP KELLER
A Gardner Looks at the Fruits of the Spirit

April 8

*Walk in love, just as Christ also
loved you and gave Himself up for us.*

EPHESIANS 5:2, NASB

God has not designed us to live like hermits in a
cave. He has designed us to live in friendship
and fellowship and community with others.
That's why the church, the body of Christ, is so
very important, for it is there that we are drawn
together in love and mutual encouragement.
We're meant to be a part of one another's lives.

—CHARLES R. SWINDOLL
Elijah

April 9

*Your word is a lamp
to my feet and a light to my path.*

PSALM 119:105

The more we know of God, the greater is our capacity to love Him. The more we love Him, the greater is our capacity to obey Him. Our new affection, however, must be made to grow. We are called to love God with our whole hearts. The new heart of flesh must be nurtured. It must be fed by the Word of God.

—R. C. SPROUL
In the Presence of God

April 10

The fear of the LORD is the beginning
of wisdom, and the knowledge
of the Holy One is understanding.

PROVERBS 9:10

It takes God to make the heart right. When I
have a wrong attitude, I look at life humanly.
When I have a right attitude, I look at life divinely.

—CHARLES R. SWINDOLL
Joseph

April 11

*If we confess our sins, He is faithful and
just to forgive us our sins and
to cleanse us from all unrighteousness.*

1 JOHN 1:9

According to Jesus, we all need forgiveness. Knowing we are inadequate before God and other people leads to compassion, but thinking we are good before God and others makes us self-centered and difficult to live with. The better we think we are, the less we can love. The more we see our need, the more we'll turn for help . . . and the more we'll help others because we're able to see their need.

—PAUL E. MILLER
Love Walked Among Us

April 12

It is He who has made us,
and not we ourselves; we are His people
and the sheep of His pasture.

PSALM 100:3

Sheep aren't the only ones who need a healing touch. We also get irritated with each other, butt heads, and then get wounded. Many of our disappointments in life begin as irritations. The large portion of our problems is not lion-sized attacks, but rather the day-to-day swarm of frustrations and mishaps and heartaches.

—MAX LUCADO
Traveling Light

April 13

*Those who know Your name will put
their trust in You; for You, LORD, have not
forsaken those who seek You.*

PSALM 9:10

The tragedies most difficult to take are those
that come through the failures, ignorance,
carelessness, or hatred of other human beings.
There are times when men seem to be working
havoc with God's plans.

But God is adequate even for these situations.
In order to fly, the bird must have two wings. One
wing is the realization of our human helplessness,
the other is the realization of God's power.

—CATHERINE MARSHALL
Moments that Matter

April 14

When he comes we will be
like him, for we will see him as he really is.

1 JOHN 3:2, NLT

When the disciples saw Jesus on the Mount of
Transfiguration, they got a peek at His glory.
He was radiant, beautiful, magnificent. He was
Jesus, the Jesus they knew and loved—only *more so*.
And we shall be glorious as well. Jesus called
Himself the Son of Man to state clearly that He is
what mankind was meant to be. What we see in
Jesus is our personal destiny.

—JOHN ELDREDGE
The Journey of Desire

April 15

*The children of men put their trust under
the shadow of Your wings.*

PSALM 36:7

When placed in the light of our awesome God,
our lives find new perspective:
Anxiety is replaced by hope when we see that
nothing could ever be bigger than God.
Fear loses its strength when we recognize that
God's power and love are a million times
greater than our weakness and failure.
Peace floods our lives when we remember that
all our needs are safely encompassed by
God's brilliant sufficiency.

—ALICIA BRITT CHOLE
Pure Joy

April 16

Through love serve one another.

GALATIANS 5:13

The world urges us to "get, get, get." Christ comes along and says, "Give, give, give." The world says happiness lies in everything from sex to spaghetti. Christ comes along and says our serenity is in knowing Him. The world says make a big splash and show your success by your possessions—impress people. Christ comes along and says the greatest among us is the one who is willing to be a servant.

—PHILLIP KELLER
A Gardner Looks at the Fruits of the Spirit

April 17

*He shall stand and feed
His flock in the strength of the LORD.*

MICAH 5:4

I have often thought of Jesus' words when He was only hours removed from the cross. In His prayer to the Father, . . . He said, "I glorified Thee on the earth, having accomplished the work which Thou hast given Me to do" (John 17:4). A little over thirty-three years after His arrival in Bethlehem, there He stood in Jerusalem, saying, in effect, "It's a wrap." He had done everything the Father sent Him to do . . . and in the final analysis, that's what mattered.

—CHARLES R. SWINDOLL
Day by Day

April 18

If any of you is having troubles, he should pray.

JAMES 5:13, NCV

Have you taken your disappointments to God? You've shared them with your neighbor, your relatives, your friends. But have you taken them to God?

Before you go anywhere else with your disappointments, go to God.

—MAX LUCADO
Traveling Light

April 19

Seek first the kingdom of God
and His righteousness, and all these things
shall be added to you.

MATTHEW 6:33

When you live to please God and to keep the inner person healthy, you discover that life gradually becomes *unified*. Instead of running here and there, trying to do everything and please everybody, you calmly face the challenges of each day without feeling pulled apart. You find it's much easier to make decisions because life is centered on one thing: seeking first "the kingdom of God and His righteousness."

—WARREN W. WIERSEBE
The Twenty Essential Qualities

April 20

*I have come down from heaven,
not to do My own will, but the will of
Him who sent Me.*

JOHN 6:38

I'm a list person. Are you? I make my daily list, my weekly list, and my monthly list. I just *love* lists.

Jesus also was a list maker. His list only had one thing on it: to do the will of His Father. You never see Him check things off His list because His list was His lifestyle. His whole life was a ministry of interruptions—on His way to the cross.

—ESTHER BURROUGHS
Splash the Living Water

*What does the LORD require of you
but to do justly, to love mercy, and to walk
humbly with your God?*

MICAH 6:8

Lists are everywhere. The publishing world has
its best-seller list, the music world its gold and
platinum album lists, the financial world its
Fortune 500 list.

The prophet Micah lists the absolute basics
"required" by the Lord. It's not a long list. In fact it's
short and simple. So the next time you feel that
living for God is getting too complicated, blow the
dust off Micah's list: to do justice, to love kindness,
to walk humbly with God.

—CHARLES R. SWINDOLL
Day by Day

April 22

He will again have compassion on us,
and will subdue our iniquities. You will cast all our
sins into the depths of the sea.

MICAH 7:19

A Christian *can* sin, but a Christian does not
have to sin.

That's an important distinction for you to
understand. You *may* commit sin and fall into
error. But that's not an automatic certainty.
You can develop a new heart to the point that
you do *not* sin. . . .

When you accept the Lord Jesus into your life,
God puts a new will within your will. He puts a
new spirit inside your spirit.

—LARRY LEA
Wisdom: The Gift Worth Seeking

April 23

Give all your worries to
him, because he cares for you.

1 PETER 5:7, NCV

Maybe you don't want to trouble God with
your hurts. *After all, He's got famines and
pestilence and wars; He won't care about my little
struggles,* you think. Why don't you let Him decide
that? He cared enough about a wedding to provide
the wine. He cared enough about Peter's tax
payment to give him a coin. He cared enough
about the woman at the well to give her answers.

—MAX LUCADO
Traveling Light

April 24

*You, LORD, are good and ready
to forgive, and abundant in
mercy to all those who call upon You.*

PSALM 86:5

Once we know that nothing we have ever done can get God to reject us because of what we are, we feel free to forgive ourselves for whatever we have *done*. And each time we forgive ourselves we pull our feet out of yesterday's failure and begin to hope again for tomorrow's blessings.

—LEWIS SMEDES
Keeping Hope Alive

April 25

I acknowledged my sin to You,
and my iniquity I have not hidden.

PSALM 32:5

When we repent, God promises restitution and forgiveness through the blood of Jesus Christ. He does not promise relief from any and all consequences, but He promises a relief that only the Spirit of God can give.

—CHARLES R. SWINDOLL
Day by Day

April 26

I am the good shepherd.
The good shepherd gives His life for the sheep.
JOHN 10:11

Real meaning to your life is found in the glorious dawn of God's story, which breaks into full revelation in the Person of Jesus Christ.

Because He emptied Himself of all but love, *you can be filled.*

Because His body was broke, *your life can be whole.*

Because His blood was shed, *your sin can be forgiven.*

Because He finished His Father's work, *your life has worth.*

—ANNE GRAHAM LOTZ
God's Story

April 27

When you pass through the waters,
I will be with you; and through the rivers,
they shall not overflow you.

ISAIAH 43:2

God does not whisk us at once to Glory. We go on living in a fractured world, suffering in one way or another the effects of sin—sometimes our own, sometimes others'. Yet I have come to understand even suffering, through the transforming power of the Cross, as a gift, for in this broken world, *in our sorrow*, He gives us Himself. *In our loneliness* He comes to meet us.

—ELISABETH ELLIOT
The Path of Loneliness

April 28

*The sacrifices of God are a broken spirit,
a broken and a contrite heart—
these, O God, You will not despise.*

PSALM 51:17

Jesus told the parable of the Prodigal Son to
dramatize what He meant by the word *repent*.
When the Prodigal Son repented he didn't just sit
still and feel sorry about all his sins. He wasn't
passive and limp about it. He didn't stay where he
was, surrounded by the swine. He got up and left!
He turned his feet in the other direction. He
sought out his father and humbled himself before
him, and then he was forgiven.

—BILLY GRAHAM
Peace with God

April 29

If any of you lacks wisdom,
let him ask of God, who gives to all liberally . . .
and it will be given to him.

JAMES 1:4

God is not only wise, He is the ground of wisdom. He is not only beautiful, He is the source and standard of all beauty. He is not merely good, He is the norm of all goodness.

He is the source, the ground, the norm, the fountainhead of all love.

—R. C. SPROUL
Loved By God

April 30

*The throne of God and of the Lamb shall be in it,
and His servants shall serve Him.*

REVELATION 22:3

Many people ask, "Well, what will we do in heaven? Just sit down and enjoy the luxuries of life?" No. The Bible indicates that we will serve God. There will be work to do for God. Our very beings will praise God.

It will be a time of total joy, service, laughter, signing, and praise to God. Imagine serving Him forever and never growing tired!

—BILLY GRAHAM
Peace with God

May

❧

Because God's promises are always true,
you can have hope!

ANNE GRAHAM LOTZ

May 1

I will not forget you. See, I have inscribed
you on the palms of My hands.

ISAIAH 49:15-16

D id you think God's silence in your life meant
He had forgotten you? Oh, no! God says He
has engraved your name on the palms of His
hands. He says that a mother could forget her
nursing baby at mealtime before He could forget
you! You are in God's heart and on His mind
every moment. He is fully informed of your
circumstances and will bring about change when
He knows the time is right.

—ANNE GRAHAM LOTZ
God's Story

May 2

My soul shall be joyful in my God; for
He has clothed me with the garments of salvation.

ISAIAH 61:10

Joy has always been one of the most significant hallmarks of God's people. It is a unique quality of character often confused with happiness.

Joy and happiness are not the same. Each springs from a totally different source.

Happiness comes from the world around me. Joy originates directly with the Spirit of the Living God.

—PHILLIP KELLER
A Gardner Looks at the Fruits of the Spirit

May 3

*God will always give [His people] what is right,
and he will not be slow to answer them.*

LUKE 18:7, NCV

When we come to God, we make requests; we don't make demands. We come with high hopes and a humble heart. We state what we want, but we pray for what is right. And if God gives us the prison of Rome instead of the mission of Spain, we accept it because we *know* "God will always give what is right to his people."

We go to Him. We bow before Him, and we *trust* in Him.

—MAX LUCADO
Traveling Light

May 4

*May [He] establish your hearts
blameless in holiness before our God.*

1 THESSALONIANS 3:13

No matter how soiled your past, no matter how snarled your present, no matter how hopeless your future seems to be—there is a way out. There is a sure, safe, everlasting way out—but there is only one! You have only one choice to make.

You can go on being miserable, discontented, frightened and unhappy. Or you can decide now to become the person Jesus promised you could be.

—BILLY GRAHAM
Peace with God

May 5

*The fruit of the Spirit is
in all goodness, righteousness, and truth.*

EPHESIANS 5:9

When Jesus left the earth, He gave us the Comforter, the Counselor, the very presence of God. When the Holy Spirit fills you, it is as if Jesus Himself takes the helm of your life and navigates your course.

When you elect the guidance system called the Holy Spirit, your life moves in the right direction. You are filled with the powerful sense of being deeply loved, since *everything* about Jesus' teaching focuses on love. You know you have enormous worth as a human being.

—NEIL CLARK WARREN
God Said It, Don't Sweat It

May 6

*You are our Father; we are the clay, and You
our potter; and all we are the work of Your hand.*

ISAIAH 64:8

God is the Potter, we are the clay. He is the one
who gives the commands; we are the ones who
obey. He never has to explain Himself; He never
has to ask permission. He is shaping us over into
the image of His Son, regardless of the pain and
heartache that may require. Those lessons are
learned a little easier when we remember that we
are not in charge, He is.

—CHARLES R. SWINDOLL
Day by Day

May 7

*In the beginning was the Word, and
the Word was with God, and the Word was God.
He was in the beginning with God.*

JOHN 1:1-2

Jesus is the living expression of what is on God's
mind. But He is more. He is the living expression
of what is on God's heart. But He is even more.
He is the very heart of the Almighty God of the
universe laid bare for all to see!

Do you want to know what is on the mind of
God? Then look at Jesus! Do you want to know the
will of God? The look at Jesus! Do you want to know
what is in the heart of God? *Then look at Jesus!*

—ANNE GRAHAM LOTZ
Just Give Me Jesus

May 8

*He has made His wonderful works
to be remembered; the LORD is gracious and
full of compassion.*

PSALM 111:4

God always does what is right because . . . that
is all He is able to do. He can only do what is
right because in His being He is altogether
righteous. Because God is love, He is loving in His
nature, and all of His actions reflect that love.

—R. C. SPROUL
Loved By God

May 9

If we are faithless, He remains faithful;
He cannot deny Himself.

2 TIMOTHY 2:13

Our moods may shift, but God's doesn't.
Our minds may change, but God's doesn't.
Our devotion may falter, but God's never does.
Even if we are faithless, He is faithful, for He
cannot betray himself. He is a sure God.

—MAX LUCADO
Traveling Light

May 10

*By faith we understand that the worlds
were framed by the word of God,
so that the things which are seen were not
made of things which are visible.*

HEBREWS 11:3

Faith motivates us to do the will of God. Note the verbs in Hebrews 11: Abel offered an acceptable sacrifice; Noah prepared an ark; Abraham went out; Abraham offered his son; Moses chose Israel over Egypt; and so on. True faith isn't feeling good about what God says; it's *doing* what God says. Faith isn't discussing the will of God; it's obeying the will of God.

— WARREN W. WIERSEBE
The Twenty Essential Qualities

May 11

*It is God . . . who has shown in our hearts to
give the light of the knowledge of the glory of God.*

2 CORINTHIANS 4:6

We do not understand many mysteries, but we accept by faith the fact that at the moment we repent of sin and turn by faith to Jesus Christ we are born again.

It is the infusion of divine life into the human soul, . . . whereby we become the children of God. We receive the breath of God. Christ through the Holy Spirit takes up residence in our hearts. We are attached to God for eternity.

—BILLY GRAHAM
Peace with God

May 12

*God is love, and he who abides
in love abides in God, and God in him.*

1 JOHN 4:16

Rigid love is not true love. It is veiled
manipulation, a conditional time bomb that
explodes when frustrated. Genuine love willingly
waits! It isn't pushy or demanding. While it has its
limits, its boundaries are far-reaching. It neither
clutches nor clings. Real love is not shortsighted,
selfish, or insensitive. It detects needs and does
what is best for the other person without being told.

—CHARLES R. SWINDOLL
Day by Day

May 13

*The LORD God will cause righteousness
and praise to spring forth before all the nations.*

ISAIAH 61:11

Joy is one of the grand attributes of God Himself.
It is an integral part of His character. Joy runs
like a sparkling stream of great good will through
His makeup. Known as the God of all joy, He
rejoices in all His own accomplishments. He is
joyful in His own delectable character.

When we discover for ourselves that God our
Father really is like this it endears Him to us in a
delightful way.

—PHILLIP KELLER
A Gardner Looks at the Fruits of the Spirit

Cast your burden on the LORD,
and He shall sustain you; He shall never permit the
righteous to be moved.

PSALM 55:22

From the world's perspective, there are many places you can go to find comfort. But there is only one place you will find a hand to catch your tears and a heart to listen to your every longing. True peace comes only from God. Nothing is so great that God is not greater still.

Is urgency in your heart? Something that threatens your emotional well-being as well as your ability to perform in life? Take it to Jesus.

—CHARLES STANLEY
Into His Presence

May 15

I sought the LORD, and He
heard me, and delivered me from all my fears.

PSALM 34:4

God creates mankind for intimacy with Himself,
as His beloved. We see it right at the start,
when He gives us the highest freedom of all—the
freedom to reject Him. The reason is obvious: love
is possible only when it is freely chosen. True love is
never constrained; our hearts cannot be taken
by force.

—JOHN ELDREDGE
The Journey of Desire

May 16

*Call to Me, and I will answer you,
and show you great and mighty things,
which you do not know.*

JEREMIAH 33:3

Swings give a feeling of weightlessness—for a
few moments you bypass the laws of gravity.
For a few moments you fly!

Dreams do much the same thing. Dreams
crash the confines of what is and what has been.
As our minds dare to see the unseen, our
imagination fuels our faith and we begin to trust
God for something more.

Some folks are afraid to dream. But connected
to God, it is safe to dream. There is freedom to let
faith take wings.

—ALICIA BRITT CHOLE
Pure Joy

May 17

Surely goodness and mercy shall follow me
all the days of my life; and I will
dwell in the house of the LORD forever.

PSALM 23:6

What a huge statement. Look at the size of it!
Goodness and mercy follow the child of God
each and every day! Think of the days that lie
ahead. What do you see? Days at home with only
toddlers? God will be at your side. Days in a
dead-end job? He will walk you through. Days
of loneliness? He will take your hand. Surely
goodness and mercy shall follow me—not some,
not most, not nearly all—but all the days of my life.

—MAX LUCADO
Traveling Light

May 18

*Blessed be the God and Father of
our Lord Jesus Christ, who . . . has begotten us
again to a living hope.*

1 PETER 1:3

There's a sense of stability in trusting the Lord.
That's how we wait silently and with a sense
of confidence. When we wait for God to direct our
steps, He does! When we trust Him to meet our
needs, He will!

—CHARLES R. SWINDOLL
Day by Day

May 19

The LORD is my shepherd;
I shall not want.

PSALM 23:1

W hat is it like to know that no matter how
messed up you might be, the good shepherd
looks at you with love, surrounds you with His
compassion, envelops you in His arms, and cares
for the details of your life? Love begins, not with
loving, but with being loved. Being loved gives you
the freedom and the resources to love. We can only
give what we have received.

—PAUL E. MILLER
Love Walked Among Us

May 20

*You will seek the LORD your God,
and you will find Him if you seek Him with all your
heart and with all your soul.*

DEUTERONOMY 4:29

Do you know God?

If Adam knew Him as a beloved Father,
if Abraham knew Him as a Friend, if Moses knew
Him as a Redeemer, if David knew Him as his
Shepherd, if Daniel knew Him as the Lion Tamer, if
Mary Magdalene knew Him as the Bondage Breaker,
if Martha knew Him as the Promise Keeper, surely
you and I can know Him too!

—ANNE GRAHAM LOTZ
Just Give Me Jesus

May 21

*In all these things we are more
than conquerors through Him who loved us.*

ROMANS 8:37

E ven after generations of people had spit in His
face, God still loved them. After a nation of
chosen ones had stripped Him naked and ripped
His incarnated flesh, He still died for them. And
even today, after billions have chosen to prostitute
themselves before the pimps of power, fame, and
wealth, He still waits for them.

It *is* inexplicable. It doesn't have a drop of logic
nor a thread of rationality. And yet, it is that very
irrationality that gives the gospel its greatest
defense. For only God could love like that.

—MAX LUCADO
God Came Near

May 22

Though your sins are like scarlet, they
shall be as white as snow.

ISAIAH 1:18

If we were declared 99.9% righteous, some verses
would have to be rewritten. Like Isaiah 1:18,
which might then read: "Come now, and let us
reason together," says the LORD, "though your sins
are as scarlet, they will be light pink."

Nonsense! The promise of sins forgiven is all
or nothing.

—CHARLES R. SWINDOLL
Day by Day

May 23

*Let the peace of God rule
in your hearts.*

COLOSSIANS 3:15

The Greek word "rule" in this verse means "on
top of everything else." It's the idea of
something being the best.

In the first century this word was used to
describe the kind of authority a judge had in a
court of law or an umpire today has on an athletic
field. Paul meant that the peace of God in our lives
should act as a judge or an umpire when it comes
to knowing God's will. When we have to make a
decision or we're struggling about what to do, we
should let the peace of God have a final say.

—JOHN HULL AND TIM ELMORE
Pivotal Praying

May 24

Who shall bring a charge against God's elect?
It is God who justifies.

ROMANS 8:33

Your sins have been forgiven. God has buried
them in the depths of the sea and placed them
behind His back of forgetfulness. Every sin is
completely wiped out. You stood before God as a
debtor, you received your discharge, you have
become reconciled to God. You are now a child
of God.

—BILLY GRAHAM
Peace with God

May 25

*We shall not all sleep, but we shall
all be changed—in a moment, in the twinkling
of an eye, at the last trumpet.*

1 CORINTHIANS 15:51-52

When Jesus went home he left the back door open. As a result, "we will all be changed— in a moment, in the twinkling of an eye."

The first moment of transformation went unnoticed by the world. But you can bet your sweet September the second one won't. The next time you use the phrase "just a moment..." remember that's all the time it will take to change this world.

—MAX LUCADO
God Came Near

May 26

*All things were made through Him, and
without Him nothing was made that was made.*

JOHN 1:3

God created atoms and angels and ants,
crocodiles and chiggers and clouds, diamonds
and dust and dinosaurs, raindrops and sweat drops,
dewdrops and blood drops, and me! And you!

The greatness of His power to create and
design and form and mold and make and build
and arrange defies the limits of our imagination.
And since He created everything, there is nothing
beyond His power to fix or mend or heal or restore.

—ANNE GRAHAM LOTZ
Just Give Me Jesus

May 27

The just shall live by faith.

ROMANS 1:17

F aith actually means surrender and commitment
to the claims of Christ. It means an
acknowledgment of sin and a turning to Christ.
We do not know Christ through the five physical
senses, but we know Him through the sixth sense
that God has given every person—that ability
to believe.

—BILLY GRAHAM
Peace with God

May 28

*Oh, taste and see that the LORD
is good. Blessed is the man who trusts in Him!*

PSALM 34:8

Taste the Lord. It's an unusual invitation.

The Hebrew word for *taste* means "to taste or eat, to discern, perceive, evaluate." The idea is of tasting something to see whether it's good to eat for sustenance and strength.

Taste life with God, and see how good it is. It's a life of blessed fulfillment.

—PETER WALLACE
What the Psalmist Is Saying to You

May 29

We love Him because He first loved us.

1 JOHN 4:19

Jesus. . . . Have you seen Him? Those who first did were never the same.

"My Lord and my God!" cried Thomas.

"I have seen the Lord," exclaimed Mary Magdalene.

"We have seen His glory," declared John.

But Peter said it best. "We were eyewitnesses of His majesty."

All the splendor of heaven revealed in a human body.

—MAX LUCADO
God Came Near

I will never leave you nor forsake you.

HEBREWS 13:5

The Love that calls us into being, woos us to Himself, makes us His bride, lays down His life for us, and daily crowns us with loving-kindness and tender mercy, will *not*, no matter how it may appear in our loneliness, abandon us. "I will never [the Greek has five different negatives here], never, never, never, never leave you or forsake you."

—ELISABETH ELLIOT
The Path of Loneliness

May 31

You are God, ready to pardon,
gracious and merciful.

NEHEMIAH 9:17

D on't get stuck on where you *were*. Don't waste
your time focusing on *what you used to be*.
Remember, the hope we have in Christ means
there's a brighter tomorrow. The sins are forgiven.
The shame is canceled out. We're no longer
chained to a deep, dark pit of the past. Grace gives
us wings to soar beyond it.

—CHARLES R. SWINDOLL
Paul: A Man of Grace and Grit

June

❧

Trusting God is doing the
greatest thing anybody can do.
ELISABETH ELLIOT

June 1

The LORD also will be a refuge . . .
in times of trouble.

PSALM 9:9

*R*efuge. A shelter from danger or trouble.
A place to go for safety.

Run to the outstretched arms of the Lord.
For He will wrap you up in His love, surround you
with His power, and protect you.

He is *your* refuge. And He is waiting to
welcome you.

— PETER WALLACE
What the Psalmist Is Saying to You

June 2

He will love you and
bless you and multiply you.

DEUTERONOMY 7:13

God is the Good Gardener who toils over us and tends us with constant care. Patiently He waits for the full fruitage. He finds joy in the planting He has done and waits eagerly for a crop. With great joy He gathers the harvest.

There is a deep delight in all He does. There is enthusiasm in everything He undertakes. There is sweet satisfaction in all His enterprises. His life, vitality, and energy are transmitted directly to me by His Spirit who resides within.

—PHILLIP KELLER
A Gardner Looks at the Fruits of the Spirit

*His divine power has given to us all things
that pertain to life and godliness,
through the knowledge of Him who called us
by glory and virtue.*

2 PETER 1:3

God is bigger than we think and greater than we think. Nothing is beyond His ability, whether it's a problem to solve, a marriage to reconcile, a memory to heal, a guilty conscience to cleanse, or a sin to forgive.

If God has the power to create and sustain the universe, *how can you think His power is insufficient for you?* He is more than able to sustain your marriage and your ministry, your faith and your finances, your hope and your health.

—ANNE GRAHAM LOTZ
Just Give Me Jesus

*"I will feed My flock, and I will
make them lie down," says the LORD God.*

EZEKIEL 34:15

There is not a hint of one person who was afraid
to draw near Jesus. There were those who
mocked Him. There were those who were envious
of Him. There were those who misunderstood
Him. There were those who revered Him. But there
was not one person who considered Him too holy,
too divine, or too celestial to touch. *There was not
one person who was reluctant to approach Him for
fear of being rejected.*

—MAX LUCADO
God Came Near

*Neither death nor life, nor angels
nor principalities nor powers, nor things present nor
things to come, nor height nor depth,
nor any other created thing, shall
be able to separate us from the love of God.*

ROMANS 8:38-39

I n this passage the apostle sets forth the
principle that gripped the reformers of the
sixteenth century: *Deus pro nobis*, which means
simply "God for us." The source of Christian
comfort is that God is for us and is on our side.
To know that God is for us is to know that no one
and nothing can ever prevail against us.

—R. C. SPROUL
Loved By God

June 6

Draw near to God and
He will draw near to you.

JAMES 4:8

S ome people find it easier to draw closer to God
in magnificent buildings and with some form
of ritual. Others find they can seek God only in
stark simplicity. Some people find themselves more
comfortable with formality, others feel more at
home with informality. The important thing is not
how we do it, but the sincerity and depth of purpose
with which we do it.

—BILLY GRAHAM
Peace with God

If you forgive men their trespasses,
your heavenly Father will also forgive you.

MATTHEW 6:14

Prayerfully letting go of wrongs or injustices
caused by others is hard. But if we're to
experience God's best for our lives, we have to learn
to let go. Letting go and allowing God to work
toward healing our wounds will bring peace of
mind and clarity of conscience. Letting go means
forgiving. Plain and simple. The Greek word for
forgive means "to let go."

—JOHN HULL AND TIM ELMORE
Pivotal Praying

June 8

Is anyone among you suffering?
Let him pray ... and the Lord will raise him up.

JAMES 5:13-15

Depression is a gloomy mindset that from time to time smudges our moods. At one time or another it afflicts us all. The waves of depression crash upon the shores of our lives in ever-increasing surges.

But is it hopeless? No. Christ is always the key to winning over our dour moods. The issue of our wholeness lies in making Christ the Lord over all circumstances.

—CALVIN MILLER
Into the Depths of God

June 9

The ways of man are before the eyes
of the LORD, and He ponders all his paths.

PROVERBS 5:21

All Abraham knew was that God wanted him to move. He didn't have a clue about the final destination. Nothing about the weather or the crime rate in the area. No information about the neighborhood he'd live in or the problems he would have to face. Nothing. He knew only that God had told him to go.

If you're waiting on God to fill in all the shading in your picture, you will never take the first step in obeying His will. You must be prepared to trust His plan, *knowing* it will be full of surprises.

—CHARLES R. SWINDOLL
Paul: A Man of Grace and Grit

June 10

When Your words came, I ate them;
they were my joy and my heart's delight, for I bear Your
name, O Lord God Almighty.

JEREMIAH 15:16, NIV

For me, good company enriches any meal.

And Jeremiah felt the same way. His favorite food was God's Word in the company of . . . God Himself!

What an incredible banquet God gives us through His Word. The Scriptures, when ingested, bring delight to our hearts and energy to our spirits. God's Word is thoroughly nutritious and always fresh.

—ALICIA BRITT CHOLE
Pure Joy

June 11

Whoever desires to save his life will lose it,
but whoever loses his life for My sake will find it.

MATTHEW 16:25

I believe the secret of happiness lies imbedded in those words, painful though they appear to be. I have observed that when any of us embarks on the pursuit of happiness for ourselves, it eludes us. Often I've asked myself why. It must be because happiness comes to us only as a dividend. When we become absorbed in something demanding and worthwhile above and beyond ourselves, happiness seems to be there as a by-product of self-giving.

—CATHERINE MARSHALL
Moments that Matter

June 12

The number of God's years
is unsearchable.

JOB 36:26, NCV

W e may search out the moment the first wave slapped on a shore or the first star burst in the sky, but we'll never find the first moment when God was God, for there is no moment when God was not God. He has never *not been*, for He is eternal. God is not bound by time.

—MAX LUCADO
He Chose the Nails

Show me Your ways, O LORD;
teach me Your paths.

PSALM 25:4

The path of peace which God's Word instructs us to pursue is not strewn with rose petals. It's a tough trail tramped out with a humble heart and lowly spirit.

Peace is the spirit and soul of persons so imbued with the presence of God's Gracious Spirit that they are not easily provoked. It is the quiet, potent, gracious attitude of serenity and good will that meets the angry onslaught of others with good cheer, equanimity, and strong repose.

—PHILLIP KELLER
A Gardner Looks at the Fruits of the Spirit

June 14

For this is God, our God forever and ever;
He will be our guide even to death.

PSALM 48:14

We live in a culture that regularly confuses humanity with deity. It's the kind of sloppy theology that suggests God sits on the edge of heaven thinking, *Wonder what they'll do next?* How absurd! God is omniscient. This implies, clearly, God never learns anything, our sinful decision and evil deeds notwithstanding. Nothing ever surprises Him. From the moment we're conceived to the moment we die, we remain safely within the frame of His watchful gaze as well as His sovereign plan.

—CHARLES R. SWINDOLL
Paul: A Man of Grace and Grit

June 15

I thank you, High God—you're breathtaking!
Body and soul, I am marvelously made!

PSALM 139:14, *THE MESSAGE*

God wanted to show the world something of His strength. Is He not a great warrior? Has He not performed the daring rescue of His beloved? And this is why He gave us the sculpture that is man. Men bear the image of God in their dangerous, yet inviting strength. Women, too, bear the image of God, but in a much different way. Is not God a being of great mystery and beauty? Is there not something tender and alluring about the essence of the Divine? And this is why He gave us the sculpture that is woman.

—JOHN ELDREDGE
The Journey of Desire

June 16

The joy of the LORD is your strength.

NEHEMIAH 8:10

One of the characteristics of the Christian is an inward joy that does not depend upon circumstances.

S. D. Gordon, said of joy: "Joy is distinctly a Christian word and a Christian thing. It is the reverse of happiness. Happiness is the result of what happens of an agreeable sort. Joy has its springs deep down inside. And that spring never runs dry, no matter what happens." Only Jesus gives that joy.

—BILLY GRAHAM
Peace with God

June 17

For He is our God, and we are the people of His pasture, and the sheep of His hand.

PSALM 95:7

When the devil comes to tell you about your past, tell him about his past—that he was cast out of heaven and defeated by the blood of Jesus Christ shed on the cross of Calvary.

When the devil comes to taunt you and to paint a negative picture about your future, tell him about his future—that he will burn in the lake of fire forever and that he will never be allowed back into heaven, where you will be spending all of eternity.

—LARRY LEA
Wisdom: The Gift Worth Seeking

June 18

*Of His fullness we have all received,
and grace for grace.*

JOHN 1:16

As children of God, we are the primary recipients of His blessing.

When the Mediterranean Sea evaporates or runs low, the Atlantic Ocean rushes in at the Strait of Gibraltar to replenish it and keep it full. When you and I are related to Jesus Christ, our strength and wisdom and peace and joy and hope may run out, but His life rushes in to keep us filled to the brim.

—ANNE GRAHAM LOTZ
Just Give Me Jesus

June 19

*God is not the author
of confusion but of peace.*

1 CORINTHIANS 14:33

At times God's plan will frighten you. Or you'll
be intimidated by its demands. Other times
you'll be disappointed. For instance, when God tells
you no, to wait, or to sit tight, you'll want to argue.
You may decide to fight. You might attempt to
negotiate. You may become angry. But when your
faith kicks in gear, none of those impulses will
control you. Faith says, "I can do this. I trust you,
Lord. I don't understand everything, but I trust
you completely."

—CHARLES R. SWINDOLL
Paul: A Man of Grace and Grit

June 20

*His compassions fail not. They are
new every morning; great is Your faithfulness.*
LAMENTATIONS 3:22-23

Some of us know very little of suffering, but we know disappointments and betrayals and losses and bitterness. Are we really meant to thank God for such things? Let's be clear about one thing. God does not cause all the things we don't like. But He does permit them to happen because it is in this fallen world that we humans must learn to walk by faith. He doesn't leave us to ourselves, however. He shares every step.

—ELISABETH ELLIOT
Keep a Quiet Heart

Be of good comfort, be of one mind,
live in peace; and the God of love and
peace will be with you.

2 CORINTHIANS 13:11

Marriage is a holy bond because it permits two people to help each other work out their spiritual destinies. God declared marriage to be good because He knew that man needed a helpmate and woman needed a protector. He desires that husbands and wives never lose sight of the original purpose of marriage. It is woman's role to love and help and reassure her husband in every way she can, and it is man's role to love and protect and provide for his wife and the children she bears, so that the home may be filled with God's peace and harmony.

—BILLY GRAHAM
Peace with God

June 22

Your Redeemer is the Holy One
of Israel; He is called the God of the whole earth.

ISAIAH 54:5

We wonder with so many miraculous testimonies around us, how we could escape God. But somehow we do. We live in an art gallery of divine creativity and yet are content to gaze only at the carpet.

The next time you hear a baby laugh or see an ocean wave, take note. Pause and listen as His Majesty whispers ever so gently, "I'm here."

—MAX LUCADO
God Came Near

June 23

You know me inside and out, . . .
You know exactly how I was made, bit by bit.

PSALM 139:15, NASB

The psalmist says that our Master Designer knew all about us from the time we were formed in our mother's womb, and even before we were born. He knew all the days of our individual lives.

We can't begin to number the precious thoughts He has about us—they number more than the grains of sand. (You will never find this kind of guarantee on the designer dress labels of the clothes you wear.)

—ESTHER BURROUGHS
Splash the Living Water

June 24

O LORD, how manifold are Your works!
In wisdom You have made them all. The earth
is full of Your possessions.

PSALM 104:24

The only way to describe God's ongoing creative activity is *extravagant*. Thunderclouds gather over the prairies, and afterward He scatters the wildflowers as far as the eye can see. He fills the oceans with orcas and urchins and who knows what. A single maple leaf is woven with greater intricacy than the finest French lace—even though it will fall with the winds of autumn. New stars are born every day; a new sunset painted and swept away each night. Such magnificent generosity.

—JOHN ELDREDGE
The Journey of Desire

June 25

The LORD will give what is good....
Righteousness will go before Him, and shall
make His footsteps our pathway.

PSALM 85:12–13

God—as we all know—does not promise us everything we get it into our minds to hope for. But He does give us reason to believe that what He does promise is a commitment we can rely on. And God's commitment promises much more than possibility.

—LEWIS SMEDES
Keeping Hope Alive

June 26

I am the God of your father Abraham;
do not fear, for I am with you.

GENESIS 26:24

Hope is not what you expect; it's what you would never dream. It's a wild, improbable tale with a pinch-me-I'm-dreaming ending. It's Abraham adjusting his bifocals so he can see not his grandson, but his son. It's Moses standing in the promised land not with Aaron or Miriam at his side, but with Elijah and the transfigured Christ.

Hope is not a granted wish or a favor performed; no, it's far greater than that. It's a zany, unpredictable dependence on a God who loves to surprise us out of our socks and be there in the flesh to see our reaction.

—MAX LUCADO
God Came Near

June 27

*If you abide in me, and my words
abide in you, ask for whatever you wish,
and it will be done for you.*

JOHN 15:7

This "abide in me" is the all-inclusive condition for effective intercession. It is the key for prayer in the name of Jesus. . . .

As we live this way, we develop what Thomas à Kempis calls "a familiar friendship with Jesus." We become accustomed to His face. We distinguish the voice of the true Shepherd from that of religious hucksters in the same way professional jewelers distinguish a diamond from glass imitations—by acquaintanceship. When we have been around the genuine article long enough, the cheap and the shoddy become obvious.

—RICHARD FOSTER
Prayer: Finding the Heart's True Home

June 28

*I will be merciful to their unrighteousness, and their
sins ... I will remember no more.*

HEBREWS 8:12

Wow! Now, *that* is a remarkable promise.
God doesn't just forgive, He forgets.
He erases the board. He destroys the evidence.
He burns the microfilm. He clears the computer.

He doesn't remember my mistakes. For all the
things He does do, this is one thing He refuses to
do. He refuses to keep a list of my wrongs.

—MAX LUCADO
God Came Near

June 29

*He who trusts in the
LORD, mercy shall surround him.*

PSALM 32:10

At times, God requires a season of waiting
before He sends His blessing. Then trust
becomes your greatest asset. If you don't trust God
with your need, you will cry out in fear and panic.
At one point during a storm on the Sea of Galilee,
the disciples thought they would perish. But Jesus
commanded the wind and waves to be still. He
taught those men how to trust Him even in the
most tempestuous of circumstances, and He is
teaching you to watch and wait for His
outstretched arm.

—CHARLES STANLEY
Into His Presence

June 30

*As many of you as were
baptized into Christ have put on Christ.*

GALATIANS 3:27

You read it right. We have "put on" Christ. When God looks at us He doesn't see us; He sees Christ. We "wear" Him. We are hidden in Him; we are covered by Him. As the song says "Dressed in His righteousness alone, faultless to stand before the throne."

Presumptuous, you say? Sacrilegious? It would be if it were my idea. But it isn't; it's His.

—MAX LUCADO
He Chose the Nails

July

Faith is not belief without proof but
trust without reservation.

D. ELTON TRUEBLOOD

July 1

*Every branch that bears fruit He prunes,
that it may bear more fruit.*

JOHN 15:2

Submitting to God's pruning can be painful.
Yielding requires persistent faith. We must hold
tightly to God's character with tears in our eyes.

But our Master Gardener is trustworthy. He
loves us too much to elevate *looking* good above
being good. With each cut of His "pruning knife,"
God thins our lives in order to thicken our
character.

—ALICIA BRITT CHOLE
Pure Joy

July 2

No good thing will He withhold from those who walk uprightly.

PSALM 84:11

Patience is the powerful capacity of selfless love to suffer long under adversity. It is that noble ability to bear with either difficult people or adverse circumstances without breaking down.

Over and beyond all of these, patience is that powerful attribute that enables a man or woman to remain steadfast under strain, not just standing still but pressing on.

—PHILLIP KELLER
A Gardner Looks at the Fruits of the Spirit

July 3

*Work out your own
salvation with fear and trembling.*

PHILIPPIANS 2:12

It would have been nice if God had let us order
life like we order a meal. I'll take good health
and a high IQ. I'll pass on the music skills, but give
me a fast metabolism. . . . Would've been nice.
But it didn't happen. When it came to your life on
earth, you weren't given a voice or a vote.

But when it comes to life after death, you were.
In my book that seems like a good deal. Wouldn't
you agree?

—MAX LUCADO
He Chose the Nails

July 4

*God did not send His Son into the world
to condemn the world, but that the world through Him
might be saved.*

JOHN 3:17

The word "benevolence" is derived from the combination of the Latin prefix *bene*, which means "well" or "good," and the Latin root that means "will." Together the prefix and the root mean "goodwill."

The Incarnation was an expression of the goodwill of God. His benevolent love. Christ came into the world not only by the *will* of the Father but by the *goodwill* of the Father.

—R. C. SPROUL
Loved By God

July 5

*In the fear of the LORD there is
strong confidence, and His children will
have a place of refuge.*

PROVERBS 14:26

Chances are good your life has grown more
complicated than it was ten years ago, or for
that matter, even five years ago. Over time you've
collected more and more stuff, taken on more
and more debt, accepted more and more
responsibilities. Now your spiritual well is dry.

Taking time to discover what really matters is
essential. . . . Don't wait for the doctor to say you've
got six months to live. Long before anything that
tragic becomes a reality, grow roots deep into the soil
of things that really matter.

—CHARLES R. SWINDOLL
Paul: A Man of Grace and Grit

July 6

Your faithfulness reaches to the clouds.
Your righteousness is like the great mountains.

PSALM 36:5-6

Consider God's faithfulness. His care and
concern for His children are stubborn
and unyielding. No matter what you do or what
happens to you, He will be with you forever.

Consider His righteousness. It is immense and
infinite, perfect in every way.

You can trust Him wholeheartedly for every
aspect of life.

—PETER WALLACE
What the Psalmist Is Saying to You

July 7

He who trusts in his riches will fall,
but the righteous will flourish like foliage.

PROVERBS 11:28

We come into life with empty hands—and it is
with empty hands that we leave it. Actually
we can possess nothing—no property and no
person—along the way. It is God who owns
everything, and we are but stewards of His
property during the brief time we are on earth.
Everything that we see about us that we count as
our possessions only comprises a loan from God.

—BILLY GRAHAM
Peace with God

July 8

*The statutes of the LORD are right, rejoicing
the heart; the commandment
of the LORD is pure, enlightening the eyes.*

PSALM 19:8

God has created us and our gifts for a place of His choosing," says Os Guinness, "and we will only be ourselves when we are finally there." Our creative nature is essential to who we are as human beings—as image bearers—and it brings us great joy to live it out with freedom and skill. Even if it's a simple act such as working on your photo albums or puttering in the garden—these, too, are how we have a taste of what was meant to rule over a small part of God's great kingdom.

—JOHN ELDREDGE
The Journey of Desire

July 9

*It is God who works in you both to will
and to do for His good pleasure.*

PHILIPPIANS 2:13

For the child of God the development of
patience has two enormous benefits. First it
produces within our character tremendous strength
and endurance.

Secondly, as we are patient under adversity we
discover the great faithfulness of our God in every
situation.

—PHILLIP KELLER
A Gardner Looks at the Fruits of the Spirit

July 10

Great is our LORD, and mighty in power;
His understanding is infinite.

PSALM 147:5

No means of measure can define God's limitless love. No barrier can hinder Him from pouring out His blessings.

He forgives and He forgets. He creates and He cleanses.

He restores and He rebuilds. He comforts and He carries.

He lifts and He loves. He is the God of the second chance.

—ANNE GRAHAM LOTZ
Just Give Me Jesus

July 11

*Not a word failed of any good thing
which the LORD had spoken to the house
of Israel. All came to pass.*

JOSHUA 21:45

The Word of God and the Word of God alone is the basis for our faith. It reveals the character of God and records His mighty works, both of which encourage us to believe and obey. The precepts of God reveal His will, and we can obey them by faith because God's commandments are still God's enablements. The promises of God are dependable.

—WARREN W. WIERSEBE
The Twenty Essential Qualities

July 12

Having been justified by faith,
we have peace with God.

ROMANS 5:1

Many of us have entered the Christian life by
faith. But having entered, we are inclined to
shift our ground. We come to feel that we will
become righteous (that is, remain acceptable to God)
only as we do certain things.

Yet with a concerted voice, the New Testament
writers teach that God's supreme interest is in
what we *are*, not what we do.

—CATHERINE MARSHALL
Moments that Matter

July 13

Who is the man that fears the LORD?
Him shall He teach in the way He chooses.

PSALM 25:12

I t's not fair," we say. It's not fair that I was born in
poverty or that I sing so poorly or that I run so
slowly. But the scales of life were forever tipped on
the side of fairness when God planted a tree in the
Garden of Eden. All complaints were silenced
when Adam and his descendants were given free
will, the freedom to make whatever eternal choice
we desire. Any injustice in this life is offset by the
honor of choosing our destiny in the next.

—MAX LUCADO
He Chose the Nails

July 14

*The Helper, the Holy Spirit, whom
the Father will send in My name, He will teach you all
things, and bring to your remembrance
all things that I said to you.*

JOHN 14:26

Today, many agree on what is absolutely evil and absolutely good. But in a world of ever-expanding shades of gray, we can lose confidence in our ability to distinguish where light ends and darkness begins.

Yet God always sees clearly. When faced with a specific decision, let us first look to His Word and ask a simple question: *Can I picture God smiling over this choice?*

God's Spirit will be faithful to teach us and guide us into all truth.

—ALICIA BRITT CHOLE
Pure Joy

July 15

*Let a man so consider us as servants
of Christ and stewards of the
mysteries of God. Moreover it is required in
stewards that one be found faithful.*

1 CORINTHIANS 4:1-2

Christ is the grand over-comer. By receiving
Jesus into our lives, we erect the inner bracing
that enables us to withstand the pressure of all our
outer circumstances. Welcoming Christ into our
lives, we gain the power to control life and not be
crushed by it. Yet to withstand the crush of life, we
must always be submitted to His inner lordship.
The yielded life becomes the strong life.

—CALVIN MILLER
Into the Depths of God

July 16

He bruises, but He binds up; He wounds,
but His hands make whole.

JOB 5:18

Oh, the hands of Jesus. Hands of incarnation at His birth. Hands of liberation as He healed. Hands of inspiration as He taught. Hands of dedication as He served. And hands of salvation as He died.

The same hand that stilled the seas stills your guilt.

The same hand that cleansed the Temple cleanses your heart.

The hand is the hand of God.

—MAX LUCADO
He Chose the Nails

They shall reign forever and ever.

REVELATION 22:5

Think for a moment. The One who created you and set all those loves and gifts in your heart, the One who has shaped all your life experiences (including the ones that seem to make no sense), this God has prepared a place for you that is a more than perfect fit for all your gifts and quirks and personality traits—even those you don't know you have. Christ is not joking when He says that we shall inherit the kingdom prepared for us and shall reign with Him forever.

—JOHN ELDREDGE
The Journey of Desire

July 18

Blessed are those who keep His testimonies,
who seek Him with the whole heart!

PSALM 119:2

Have you ever thought of going to church as a divine appointment? Have you ever thought of Bible study as a divine appointment? That Jesus is patiently, personally waiting to meet with you there?

What a difference it would make in our attitude of expectancy and our habit of consistency if we truly wrapped our hearts around the knowledge that each is a divine appointment; that Jesus Himself is waiting to meet with us.

—ANNE GRAHAM LOTZ
Just Give Me Jesus

July 19

Well done, good and faithful servant;
you were faithful over a few things, I will
make you ruler over many things.

MATTHEW 25:21

The Cross is a sign of loss—a shameful, humiliating, abject, total loss. Yet it was Jesus' loss that meant heavenly gain for the whole world. Although secured in a tomb with a heavy stone, a seal, and posted guards, He could not be held down by death. He came out of the grave as the Death of Death and Hell's Destruction.

His death was a new beginning. Those who accept that truth receive not only the promise of heaven, but the possibility of heaven on earth, where the Risen Christ walks with us.

—ELISABETH ELLIOT
The Path of Loneliness

July 20

*Righteousness and justice are the
foundation of Your throne; mercy and
truth go before Your face.*

PSALM 89:14

Pinning our hopes on promises always boils
down in the end to one thing: *trust in the person
who makes them.*

Trust the Maker of the universe to keep His
promises. It is the ultimate fallback hope.

—LEWIS SMEDES
Keeping Hope Alive

July 21

Whatever you do, do it heartily, as to the Lord
and not to men, knowing that from the Lord you will
receive the reward of the inheritance.

COLOSSIANS 3:23

You may be one of those individuals desperately
seeking a way off the treadmill. My advice to
you is to stop trying to be the tops in your field.
Be an excellent *whatever*. Do the very best you can
with what God has given you. If His plan includes
bringing you to higher levels of success, He'll do
that, in His time, according to His master plan.
Your part is to get out of the traffic and set your
mind on kingdom priorities—stuff that *really*
matters. God is good.

—CHARLES R. SWINDOLL
Paul: A Man of Grace and Grit

*Our light affliction, which is but for a
moment, is working for us a far more exceeding and
eternal weight of glory.*

2 CORINTHIANS 4:17

L ife is now a battle and a journey. This is the
truest explanation for what is going on, the only
way to rightly understand our experience. Life is
not a game of striving and indulgence. It is not a
long march of duty and obligation. Life is a
desperate quest through dangerous country to a
destination that is, beyond all our wildest hopes,
indescribably good.

—JOHN ELDREDGE
The Journey of Desire

July 23

Where can I flee from Your presence?
If I take the wings of the morning, and dwell in the
uttermost parts of the sea, even there
Your hand shall lead me.

PSALM 139: 7, 9

Our asking "Where is God?" is like a fish
asking "Where is water?" or a bird asking
"Where is air?" God is everywhere! Equally present in
Peking and Peoria. As active in the lives of
Icelanders as in the lives of Texans.

We cannot find a place where God is not.

—MAX LUCADO
He Chose the Nails

July 24

> *How precious is your lovingkindness,*
> *O God! Therefore the children of men put their trust*
> *under the shadow of Your wings.*

PSALM 36:7

The Hebrew word for *lovingkindness* means "unfailing love, steadfast love, mercy, goodness." God extends lovingkindness to us, His children. Like a mother hen brooding over her chicks, the Father invites you under His wings to be protected, warmed, and filled. There, you can relax and rest.

—PETER WALLACE
What the Psalmist Is Saying to You

July 25

*We are His workmanship,
created in Christ Jesus for good works.*

EPHESIANS 2:10

Although God cares about financial stability, world peace, and social justice, He has one great thing on His mind today—you. You are His workmanship, His masterpiece. There is no one else exactly like you, and God cares for you with infinite watchfulness. He knows exactly how many hairs came out in your brush this morning. Your checkbook matters as much as the federal budget, harmony in your home as much as harmony among nations.

—CHARLES STANLEY
Into His Presence

July 26

"Surely I am coming quickly."
Amen. Even so, come, Lord Jesus.

REVELATION 22:20

The Lord Jesus is coming back! That's how much He loves us. The plan of salvation is not only to satisfy us in this world and give us a new life here, but He has a great plan for the future. For eternity!

—BILLY GRAHAM
Peace with God

July 27

The eyes of the LORD run to and fro
throughout the whole earth,
to show Himself strong on behalf of those
whose heart is loyal to Him.

2 CHRONICLES 16:9

In God's kingdom, comparisons are not allowed. We make a terrible mistake comparing. God does not have a standard by which He measures us against each other. We do that. His standard is far higher. Holy God measures each of us against His Son, Jesus. That should change your focus. God will not ask if we wear specific clothing labels, He will want to know if we are clothed in Christ Jesus.

—ESTHER BURROUGHS
Splash the Living Water

July 28

Give us this day our daily bread.

MATTHEW 6:11

J esus invites us to pray for daily bread.

In doing so, He has transfigured the trivialities of everyday life. Try to imagine what our prayer experience would be like if He had forbidden us to ask for the little things. What if the only things we were allowed to talk about were the weighty matters, the important things, the profound issues? We would be orphaned in the cosmos, cold, and terribly alone. But the opposite is true; He welcomes us with our 1,001 trifles, for they are each important to Him.

—RICHARD FOSTER
Prayer: Finding the Heart's True Home

July 29

I will strengthen you, yes, I will help you.
I will uphold you with my righteous right hand.

ISAIAH 41:10

Whatever the circumstances, whatever the
call, whatever the duty, whatever the price,
whatever the sacrifice—God's strength will be
your strength in your hour of need.

—BILLY GRAHAM
Peace with God

July 30

*Be tenderhearted, be courteous ... that
you may inherit a blessing.*

1 PETER 3:8-9

Inevitably, when we stand strong and alone like
a steer in a blizzard, looking like we can make it
on our own, we easily forget that each life-
sustaining beat of our hearts is a gift from God—
we're really not that independent after all.

We not only need the Lord, we need each
other. That need only intensifies when the
barometer of life drops to the bottom of the
gauge—when the winds of adversity blow hard
against our souls. We cannot make it on our own.

—CHARLES R. SWINDOLL
Paul: A Man of Grace and Grit

I will sing of the mercies of the LORD forever;
with my mouth will I make
known Your faithfulness to all generations.

PSALM 89:1

Henri Nouwen once asked Mother Teresa for spiritual direction. "Spend one hour each day in adoration of your Lord," she said, "and never do anything you know is wrong. Follow this, and you'll be fine." Such simple, yet profound advice. Worship is the act of the abandoned heart adoring God.

—JOHN ELDREDGE
The Journey of Desire

August

*There is a delicious gladness
that comes from God.*

MAX LUCADO

August 1

*Those who wait on the LORD shall renew
their strength; they shall
mount up with wings like eagles.*

ISAIAH 40:31

Waiting is part of ordinary time. We discover
God in our waiting: waiting in checkout lines,
waiting for the telephone to ring, waiting for
graduation, waiting for a promotion, waiting to retire,
waiting to die. The waiting itself becomes prayer as
we give our waiting to God. In waiting we begin to
get in touch with the rhythms of life—stillness and
action, listening and decision. They are the rhythms
of God. It is in the everyday and the commonplace
that we learn patience, acceptance, and contentment.

—RICHARD FOSTER
Prayer: Finding the Heart's True Home

August 2

*The generous soul will be made rich,
and he who waters will also be watered himself.*

PROVERBS 11:25

Whatever we may own, whether in large or small measure, when placed gladly in God's great strong hands can be blessed and multiplied a thousand times to enrich countless other lives. If clutched tightly and timidly to our own selfish souls it will shrivel away to a mere whimsy, wasted on one's self.

—PHILLIP KELLER

A Gardner Looks at the Fruits of the Spirit

August 3

God makes his people
strong. God gives his people peace.

PSALM 29:11, THE MESSAGE

When God plans to use us, He puts us through the paces. He allows a certain amount of suffering. God may use the strong, stubborn, independent individualists in the world, but not long-term. He much prefers the humble, the broken, the bruised, the humble, even the crushed. He works much more effectively in the lives of people who've learned they can't make it on their own, especially those who acknowledge they desperately need God and others.

—CHARLES R. SWINDOLL
Paul: A Man of Grace and Grit

August 4

*All things work together for good
to those who love God, to those who are the called
according to His purpose.*

ROMANS 8:28

God didn't create you to be a failure or a sinner. He created you in Christ Jesus to be righteousness. He created you to live a life that is more abundant.

Your genetic makeup, your family history, or your past experiences don't dictate your future. God holds your future in His hands, and He has promised to work all things together for your GOOD as long as you love and trust Him.

—LARRY LEA
Wisdom: The Gift Worth Seeking

August 5

*I, the LORD, have called You in righteousness,
and will hold Your hand.*

ISAIAH 42:6

A re you filled with anxiety and worry about
some problem, wondering what will happen?
Listen: As a child of God through faith in Christ,
you can turn these over to Christ, knowing that He
loves you and is able to help you. At times He may
take the problem away; other times He may give
you strength to bear it. But you can rest in Him.

—BILLY GRAHAM
The Secret of Happiness

August 6

*Love your enemies, bless those who curse you,
do good to those who hate you.*

MATTHEW 5:44

When Jesus commands us to love our enemies, He defines that love not so much in terms of feelings of affection but in terms of actions. To love our enemies requires that we bless them when they curse us and do good to them when they hate us. This is what it means to mirror and reflect the love of God, because God does good to those who hate Him and blesses people while they are cursing Him.

—R. C. SPROUL
Loved By God

August 7

> *We are made holy through the sacrifice*
> *of his body. Christ made this sacrifice only*
> *once, and for all time.*

HEBREWS 10:10, NCV

The Son of God became the Lamb of God, the cross became the altar, and we were made holy through the sacrifice Christ made in His body once and for all time.

What needed to be paid was paid. What had to be done was done. Innocent blood was required. Innocent blood was offered, once and for all time. Bury those five words deep in your heart. *Once and for all time.*

—MAX LUCADO
He Chose the Nails

August 8

*I will dwell in them and walk
among them. I will be their God.*

2 CORINTHIANS 6:16

The Christian life is full of paradox (as if you hadn't noticed). Listen to how Paul describes his experience of the quest: "Sorrowful, yet always rejoicing; poor, yet making many rich; having nothing, and yet possessing everything" (2 Cor. 6:10, NIV). How true this is. If we will remain open to sorrow, we can know joy. Somehow being empty allows us to make others rich. And if we are willing to let go, we'll discover something most surprising—that all is ours.

—JOHN ELDREDGE
The Journey of Desire

August 9

*I am the good shepherd; and
I know My sheep, and am known by My own.*

JOHN 10:14

Jesus looked out at the approaching crowds and
saw people who were seeking God. He saw
people as more important than His own plans and
need for rest.

He saw people not as an interruption, but as
an opportunity to reveal His loving care and His
Father's compassionate power to meet their
deepest needs.

He saw people as sheep who needed a shepherd.
He saw people *as God saw them.*

—ANNE GRAHAM LOTZ
Just Give Me Jesus

*Looking unto Jesus, the author
and finisher of our faith....*

HEBREWS 12:2

Jesus is Lord, and this is the primary positive
confession that should define our lives.
Humility is our bread, obedience our wine.
We gain true humility not by putting ourselves
down but by standing next to Christ. Once we see
how great is the Savior's love for us, we know our
lovely place in the world. Humility thus gained is
power and triumph.

—CALVIN MILLER
Into the Depths of God

*You will guide me with Your
counsel, and afterward receive me to glory.*

PSALM 73:24

Very few individuals jump into exceptional
work, though most would prefer doing just
that. As soon as we walk across that stage and
receive that diploma, we're ready for the big time.
Our slick resume makes us look like a combination
of Joan of Arc, Winston Churchill, and Mother
Theresa.

But that's not God's way. He prepares His
servants most often through extended periods of
waiting, designed to hone skills and break wills,
to shape character and give depth. While He
works, we wait.

—CHARLES R. SWINDOLL
Paul: A Man of Grace and Grit

August 12

*The Son of God has come and
has given us an understanding, that we
may know Him who is true.*

1 JOHN 5:20

When you're in the middle of a bad day . . .
aim your hard questions at God, not man.
Why? Because in life's darkest hours, there are
usually no human beings with adequate answers.
Counselors may analyze, associates may sympathize,
and experienced friends may empathize. But finite
minds and feeble flesh can never satisfy us with the
Presence we seek, for we truly cry for God Himself,
not answers.

—JACK HAYFORD
How to Live Through a Bad Day

August 13

The ... ones who follow the Lamb ...
were redeemed from among men.

REVELATION 14:4

We often think of God's will as a thin, barely visible line drawn with chalk that blurs in bad weather. However, the Scriptures speak of our relationship with God as a *way*, not a line. His will is a path paved with great grace.

God does not play hide and seek with those who have committed their lives to Him. Though the specific placement of His children varies greatly, God's will for us all is quite similar. [He] simply says, "follow Me."

—ALICIA BRITT CHOLE
Pure Joy

August 14

You, O LORD, are our Father;
Our Redeemer from Everlasting.

ISAIAH 63:16

If I am willing to be still in my Master's hand,
can I not then be still in everything? He's got
the whole world *in His hands!* Never mind whether
things come from God Himself or from people—
everything comes by His ordination or permission.
If I mean to be obedient and submissive to the
Lord because He is my Lord, I must not forget that
whatever He allows to happen becomes, for *me,* His
will at that moment.

—ELISABETH ELLIOT
Keep a Quiet Heart

August 15

*All of you who were baptized into Christ
have clothed yourselves with Christ.*

GALATIANS 3:27, NIV

While on the cross, Jesus felt the indignity and disgrace of a criminal. No, He was not guilty. No, He had not committed a sin. And, no, He did not deserve to be sentenced. But you and I were, we had, and we did.

Though we come to the cross dressed in sin, we leave the cross dressed in "garments of salvation" (Isa. 61:10, NIV). Indeed, we leave dressed in Christ Himself.

—MAX LUCADO
He Chose the Nails

August 16

If by one man's offense many died,
much more the grace of God and the gift by the grace
of the one Man, Jesus Christ,
abounded to many.

ROMANS 5:15

We do not come to know God through works—
we come to know Him by faith through grace.
We cannot work our way toward happiness and
heaven; we cannot moralize our way, we cannot
reform our way, we cannot buy our way. Salvation
comes as a gift of God through Christ.

—BILLY GRAHAM
The Secret of Happiness

August 17

*The counsel of the LORD stands
forever; the plans of His heart to all generations.*

PSALM 33:11

Note the phrase "the plans of His heart." It takes care of any nightmares you may have about merciless masters, heartless robots, and faceless machines. Since the will of God comes from the heart of God, then His will is the expression of His love.

—WARREN W. WIERSEBE
The Twenty Essential Qualities

August 18

If we live in the Spirit,
let us also walk in the Spirit.

GALATIANS 5:25

The Holy Spirit is powerfully at work in your
life, hovering over your heart, preparing you to
love God. He hovers over your mind, preparing
you to understand spiritual things and the truth
of His Word. He hovers over your will, preparing
you to make decisions that are pleasing to Him.
All the powers of God—the same power that hung
the stars in place and put the planets in their
courses and transformed Earth—now resides in
you to energize and strengthen you to become the
person God created you to be.

—ANNE GRAHAM LOTZ
Just Give Me Jesus

August 19

The testing of your faith produces patience.

JAMES 1:3

I t occurs to me that I've never met anyone young
and patient. (To be honest, I've not met many old
and patient folks neither). We're all in a hurry.
We don't like to miss one panel of a revolving door.
Patience comes hard in a hurry-up society. Yet, it's
an essential quality, cultivated only in extended
periods of waiting.

—CHARLES R. SWINDOLL
Paul: A Man of Grace and Grit

*There is one God and one mediator
between God and men, the man Christ Jesus.*

1 TIMOTHY 2:5, NIV

Somewhere, sometime, somehow you got tangled up in garbage, and you've been avoiding God.

You've allowed a veil of guilt to come between you and your Father. You wonder if you could ever feel close to God again.

God welcomes you. God is not avoiding you. God is not resisting you. The door is open, and God invites you in.

—MAX LUCADO
He Chose the Nails

August 21

If we are faithless, He remains faithful.

2 TIMOTHY 2:13

There is an old saying among orchardists that "The most heavily laden branches always bow the lowest on the tree."

So it is the generosity of our God that humbles our haughty hearts. It is the depth of Christ's compassion that crumbles the tough crust around our self-centered characters. His own gentle, gracious Spirit displaces our arrogance and self-preoccupation. It leaves us laden with His fruits of lowliness and gentleness.

—PHILLIP KELLER
A Gardner Looks at the Fruits of the Spirit

August 22

*In everything give thanks; for this is the will
of God in Christ Jesus for you.*

1 THESSALONIANS 5:18

How can I deal with resentments that smolder inside me? The verse above holds the answer. I am to praise God for *all* things, regardless of where they seem to originate. Doing this, He points out, is the key to receiving the blessings of God. Praise will wash away my resentments.

—CATHERINE MARSHALL
Moments that Matter

August 23

*I said, "I will confess my transgressions to
the LORD," and You forgave the iniquity of my sin.*

PSALM 32:5

With God, honesty is without a doubt the best
policy. Because He knows everything already.
When you commit a sin, acknowledge it to the
Lord. Don't try to hide it or stuff it or pretend it
didn't happen. It's all out in the brightness of
heaven's holy light, whether you see it or not.

When you do, the psalmist assures you of
God's forgiveness.

—PETER WALLACE
What the Psalmist Is Saying to You

August 24

*Blessed be . . . the Father of mercies
and God of all comfort, who comforts us
in all our tribulation.*

2 CORINTHIANS 1:3-4

S ometimes we just don't feel like singing or
smiling. Matter of fact, there are times it's
hypocritical to paste a smile on your face.

It is in those times that I am most thankful for
the Scriptures. In God's Word we not only discover
His will for our lives, we find words of genuine
comfort for those times when life comes unglued.

—CHARLES R. SWINDOLL
Paul: A Man of Grace and Grit

August 25

*The Lord is faithful, who will establish you
and guard you from the evil one.*

2 THESSALONIANS 3:3

Why did Jesus live on earth as long as He did?
Why not step into our world just long
enough to die for our sins and then leave? Why not
a sinless year or week? Why did He have to live a
life? To take on our sins is one thing, but to take on
our sunburns, our sore throats? To experience
death, yes—but to put up with life? To put up with
long roads, long days, and short tempers? Why did
He do it?

Because He wants you to trust Him.

—MAX LUCADO
He Chose the Nails

August 26 ✳

*You were sealed with the Holy Spirit of promise,
who is the guarantee of our inheritance.*

EPHESIANS 1:13–14

Our Holy Spirit is a Person; our Teacher, our
Guide, the One who comes along beside us.
God is committed to the task of working in us,
developing us, and deepening the character traits
of His Son in us through the Holy Spirit until we
look like Him. We are not on our own in this
process. He has given us the person of the Holy
Spirit to see that we become like Him in every way.

—ESTHER BURROUGHS
Splash the Living Water

August 27

*The peace of God, which surpasses
all understanding, will keep your
hearts and minds through Christ Jesus.*

PHILIPPIANS 4:7

The storm was raging. The sea was beating against the rocks in huge, dashing waves. The lightning was flashing, the thunder was roaring, the wind was blowing; but the little bird was asleep in the crevice of the rock, its head serenely under its wing, sound asleep.

In Christ we are relaxed and at peace in the midst of the confusions, bewilderments, and perplexities of this life. The storm rages, but our hearts are at rest.

—BILLY GRAHAM
Peace with God

August 28

*You are complete in Him, who is
the head of all principality and power.*

COLOSSIANS 2:10

True surrender is not an easy out, calling it quits early in the game. This kind of surrender comes only *after* the night of wrestling. It comes only after we open our hearts to care deeply. Then we choose to surrender, or give over, our deepest desires to God. And with them we give over our hearts, our deepest selves. The freedom and beauty and rest that follow are among the greatest of all surprises.

—JOHN ELDREDGE
The Journey of Desire

August 29

> *Let us, then, feel free to come before*
> *God's throne. Here there is grace. And we can receive*
> *mercy and grace to help us when we need it.*

HEBREWS 4:16, NCV

Don't we need someone to trust who is bigger than we are? Aren't we tired of trusting the people of this earth for understanding? Aren't we weary of trusting the things of this earth for strength? A drowning sailor doesn't call on another drowning sailor for help. A pauper knows better than to beg from another pauper. He knows he needs someone who is stronger than he is.

Jesus' message is this: I am that person. Trust Me.

—MAX LUCADO
He Chose the Nails

August 30

*Every good gift and every perfect gift is from above,
and comes down from the Father of lights.*

JAMES 1:17

Rather than racing into the limelight, we need to accept our role in the shadows. Don't promote yourself. Don't push yourself to the front. Let someone else do that. Better yet, let God do that.

If you're great, trust me, the word will get out. You'll be found . . . in God's time. If you're necessary for the plan, God will put you in the right place at just the precise time. God's work is not about us. It's His production, start to finish.

—CHARLES R. SWINDOLL
Paul: A Man of Grace and Grit

August 31

Blessed are all those who put their trust in Him.

PSALM 2:12

I n the race of life, God our heavenly Father has come alongside us through the Person of the Holy Spirit. And when we think we can't go one more step, when our hearts feel heavy, when our minds become dull, when our spirits are burned out, we have the *parakletos,* Who comes alongside us, puts His everlasting arms around us, and gently walks with us to the finish.

—ANNE GRAHAM LOTZ
Just Give Me Jesus

September

*The brightest gem in the crown
of God is His goodness.*

CHARLES SPURGEON

September 1

*God is faithful; he will not let you
be tempted beyond what you can bear.*

1 CORINTHIANS 10:13, NIV

God came down and lived in this same world as
a man. He showed us how to live in this world,
subject to its vicissitudes and necessities, that we
might be changed—not into an angel or a storybook
princess, not wafted into another world, but changed
into saints in this world. The secret is *Christ in me,*
not me in a different set of circumstances.

—ELISABETH ELLIOT
Keep a Quiet Heart

I press toward the goal for the prize
of the upward call of God in Christ Jesus.

PHILIPPIANS 3:14

God's goal is not to make sure you're happy. No matter how hard it is for you to believe this, it's time to do so. Life is not about your being comfortable and happy and successful and pain free. It is about becoming the man or woman God has called you to be.

Life is not about you! It's about God.

—CHARLES R. SWINDOLL
Paul: A Man of Grace and Grit

September 3

He who believes in Me has everlasting life.
I am the bread of life.

JOHN 6:47–48

When the disciples went into the village, they only brought back food. When the Samaritan woman went into the village, she brought back the entire village. The disciples, who knew the Bread of Life, went for physical bread. The woman, who had just met the Bread of Life, brought the hungry to the Bread of Life whom she knew as the living water.

One Messiah. One Samaritan. One village— forever changed.

—ESTHER BURROUGHS
Splash the Living Water

*May the God of peace Himself sanctify
you completely; and may your whole spirit, soul,
and body be preserved blameless.*

1 THESSALONIANS 5:23

I f we always feel good and look good and lead a
good life; if our kids always behave and our
home is always orderly and our bank account is
always sufficient and we are patient and kind and
thoughtful, others shrug because they're capable of
that, too.

On the other hand, if we have a splitting
headache, the kids are screaming, the phone is
ringing, the supper is burning yet we are still
patient, kind, and thoughtful, the world sits up and
takes notice. The world knows that kind of
behavior is not natural. It's supernatural.

—ANNE GRAHAM LOTZ
Just Give Me Jesus

September 5

*Having been justified by faith, we have peace
with God through our Lord Jesus Christ.*

ROMANS 5:1

Apart from God there is no lasting quenching of
our spiritual hunger and thirst.

Each of us was created in the image and
likeness of God. We were made for God's
fellowship, and our hearts can never be satisfied
without His communion. Just as iron is attracted
to a magnet, the soul in its state of hunger is
drawn to God.

—BILLY GRAHAM
The Secret of Happiness

September 6

*Whatever things you ask
when you pray, believe that you receive them,
and you will have them.*

MARK 11:24

With God, there is only the infinite NOW. Therefore, by faith we must grasp the fact that all the blessings we shall ever need are already deposited in the Treasury of Heaven.

Money in any checking account will stay right there until the owner cashes a check *in the present*. Even so, we shall receive God's blessings only as we claim them one by one *in the present*. Faith in the future tense is hope—not faith. A sure sign that our hope has passed into faith is when we stop begging God and begin thanking Him for the answer to our prayer.

—CATHERINE MARSHALL
Moments that Matter

September 7

*God demonstrates His own love
toward us, in that while we
were still sinners, Christ died for us.*

ROMANS 5:8

The Incarnation, the life and the death of Jesus,
answers once and for all the question, "What is
God's heart toward me?" That is why Paul says in
Romans 5, "Look here, at the Cross. Here is the
demonstration of God's heart. At the point of our
deepest betrayal, when we had run our farthest
from him and gotten so lost in the woods we could
never find our way home, God came and died to
rescue us."

—BRENT CURTIS AND JOHN ELDREDGE
The Sacred Romance

September 8

If we live, we live for the Lord; and if we die,
we die for the Lord. Whether
therefore we live or die, we belong to the Lord.

ROMANS 14:7-9, NEB

The life and death of all of us is in the same Hands. We are always surrounded by the Unseen, among whom are the angels, ministers of fire, explicitly commissioned to guard us. He who keeps us neither slumbers nor sleeps. His love is always awake, always aware, always surrounding and upholding and protecting. If a spear or a bullet finds its target in the flesh of one of His servants, it is not because of inattention on His part. It is because of love.

—ELISABETH ELLIOT
The Path of Loneliness

September 9

*Blessed is the man who ... delight[s]
in the law of the LORD. ... He shall be like a tree
planted by the rivers of water.*

PSALM 1:1-3

I f you will be faithful in meditating on the Word
of God every day ... you will have a wellspring
of joy in your life that bubbles up like an artesian
well. It will be like rivers of living water. You won't
have to run to and fro seeking to prime the pump
of your spiritual life. The life will be within you
and flowing from you.

—LARRY LEA
Wisdom: The Gift Worth Seeking

September 10

I can do all things
through Christ who strengthens me.

PHILIPPIANS 4:13

T he suffering you endure can ultimately turn to
your benefit. God is working. Only He knows
the end from the beginning, and He knows you and
your needs far better than even you do. Don't ask,
"Why is this happening to me?" Rather, ask the
question, "How should I respond?" Otherwise,
you'll miss the beneficial role suffering plays in life.

—CHARLES R. SWINDOLL
Paul: A Man of Grace and Grit

September 11

The LORD does not see as man sees;
for man looks at the outward appearance,
but the LORD looks at the heart.

1 SAMUEL 16:7

How wonderful that God calls the seemingly unqualified to serve Him. Few of us are the eldest, the brightest, the most beautiful, or the most gifted. But God does not judge us by our outward appearance. . . .

God is not distracted by style, personality, appearance, or achievement. His gaze pierces the flesh and weighs the heart. Then He places His hand upon sincere souls and turns shepherds into kings.

—ALICIA BRITT CHOLE
Pure Joy

September 12

Does not the potter have power over the clay?

ROMANS 9:21

Jesus makes suffering understandable: as the Potter, He uses suffering as the pressure on the wet "clay" of our lives. Under His gentle, loving touch, our lives are molded into a "shape" that pleases Him. But the shape that is so skillfully wrought is not enough. He not only desires our lives to be useful, He also wants our character to be radiant. And so He places us in the furnace of affliction until our "colors" are revealed—colors that reflect the beauty of His own character.

—ANNE GRAHAM LOTZ
Just Give Me Jesus

Create in me a clean heart, O God,
and renew a steadfast spirit within me.

PSALM 51:10

The late Leonard Bernstein, composer and famed conductor, was asked what he believed to be the most difficult instrument in the orchestra to play. He responded, "Second fiddle!"

When you examine the life of any great individual, you soon discover an entire section of second-fiddlers, super people, gifted in their own rights, but content to play their parts seated in the second chair.

—CHARLES R. SWINDOLL
Paul: A Man of Grace and Grit

September 14

*I am like a green olive tree
in the house of God; I trust in the mercy
of God forever and ever.*

PSALM 52:8

A tree stands in the courtyard. Immovable. Unshakable. With roots deep in the rich earth, drawing strength, support, and sustenance.

An olive tree is evergreen. Always alive, always growing, limbs spreading and greenery flourishing. That was how David pictured himself as a child of God. The question of his place in the world had been settled. He would trust in God's love forever and ever.

— PETER WALLACE
What the Psalmist Is Saying to You

September 15

*God put the wrong on him who
never did anything wrong,
so we could be put right with God.*

2 CORINTHIANS 5:21, THE MESSAGE

The blood of Christ does not cover your sins, conceal your sins, postpone your sins, or diminish your sins. It takes away your sins, once and for all time.

Jesus allows your mistakes to be lost in His perfection.

—MAX LUCADO
He Chose Nails

Blessed are the poor in spirit,
for theirs is the kingdom of heaven.

MATTHEW 5:3

Happy are the meek. Happy are the yielded. Happy are those who trustingly put their lives, their fortunes, and their futures in the capable hands of their Creator. Happy are those who "let go and let God."

—BILLY GRAHAM
The Secret of Happiness

September 17

This is the day the LORD
has made; we will rejoice and be glad in it.

PSALM 118:24

As we open our eyes each morning, God sets
before us a priceless present. Unique, fresh,
and full of potential, each day God gives us *time*.

"Rejoice!" the psalmist says. Has God granted
you another day? "Rejoice and be glad in it!" . . .

With each new day, God gives us time as a
gracious gift. Rejoice!

—ALICIA BRITT CHOLE
Pure Joy

September 18

Be merciful, just as your Father also is merciful.

LUKE 6:36

To be kind toward others is merely doing to them what we would like them to do to us. This kindness is linked to mercy. God's love is manifested by and through His mercy. Mercy is an act of kindness. It is also an expression of tenderness.

—R. C. SPROUL
Loved By God

September 19

*The heavens will praise Your wonders, O LORD; Your
faithfulness also in the assembly of the saints.*

PSALM 89:5

When God works on behalf of His people,
the world will know it. All creation will
acknowledge it.

And when God works on behalf of His people,
His angels will know it, and will praise His
faithfulness.

God is working on your behalf. He is providing
everything you need right now to live a fulfilled life.

—PETER WALLACE
What the Psalmist Is Saying to You

September 20

*God is at work within you,
helping you want to obey him, and then
helping you do what he wants.*

PHILIPPIANS 2:13, TLB

As a result of being saved, what do we do? We obey God with deep reverence and shrink back from all that might displease Him. Practically put, we love our neighbor and refrain from gossip. We refuse to cheat on taxes and spouses and do our best to love people who are tough to love. Do we do this in order to be saved? No. These are the good things that result from being saved.

—MAX LUCADO
He Chose the Nails

September 21

*God has chosen the weak things of the
world to put to shame the things which are mighty.*

1 CORINTHIANS 1:27

It is the sublime Spirit of the living God who
bestows upon us the capacity to express genuine
concern and compassion for others. His selfless
self-giving enables us to treat others with courtesy
and consideration. This quality is much more than
a thin veneer of proper propriety or superficial
politeness.

Rather, it is the epitome of a laid-down life,
poured out, lived out on behalf of others.

—PHILLIP KELLER
A Gardner Looks at the Fruits of the Spirit

September 22

*The fear of the LORD
is the beginning of knowledge.*

PROVERBS 1:7

Wisdom comes from God. It is not something inbred into human nature as an innate ability. Wisdom is a gift or a grace that comes from God, and, like all gifts from God, you must choose to receive it. It's available to you. God not only permits you to have it but also desires you to have it. You must accept it, however, and in the accepting lies a choice.

—LARRY LEA
Wisdom: The Gift Worth Seeking

September 23

*God's Word vaults across the skies from
sunrise to sunset, ... warming hearts to faith.*

PSALM 19:6, *THE MESSAGE*

When God gets into our hoping, we pin our
hopes on a Person. More exactly, on a Person
and the promises He makes. Not that He will see
to it that we get everything we wish for and believe
is possible, but that He will give us what He
promises. So now our hope moves from a belief
that the good we want is possible to a trust that
God intends to keep His promise and is competent
to do it.

—LEWIS SMEDES
Keeping Hope Alive

*The secret of the LORD is with those who
fear Him, and He will show them His covenant.*

PSALM 25:14

When we need help, we wish we knew
somebody who is wise enough to tell us what
to do, reachable when we need him, and even able
to help us. God is. Omniscient, omnipresent,
omnipotent—everything we need. The issue is
confidence in the Shepherd Himself, a confidence
so complete that we offer ourselves without any
reservation whatsoever and determine to do what
He says.

—ELISABETH ELLIOT
Keep a Quiet Heart

September 25

*Christ also suffered for us, leaving
us an example, that you should follow His steps.*

1 PETER 2:21

Jesus died . . . on purpose. No surprise.
No hesitation. No faltering. . . .

The way Jesus marched to His death leaves no
doubt: He had come to earth for this moment.

The journey to the cross didn't begin in Jericho.
It didn't begin in Galilee. It didn't begin in Nazarath.
It didn't even begin in Bethlehem. The journey to
the cross began long before. As the echo of the
crunching of the fruit was still sounding in the
garden, Jesus was leaving for Calvary.

—MAX LUCADO
And the Angels were Silent

September 26

Men have not heard nor perceived by the ear,
nor has the eye seen any God besides
You, who acts for the one who waits for Him.

ISAIAH 64:4

When you wait on the Lord for an answer, you are saying, in effect, "God, I'm here. I reverence You. I fear You with an awesome respect. I love You. And I'm waiting here in Your presence until I hear what You want me to do."

—LARRY LEA
Wisdom: The Gift Worth Seeking

September 27

*You, O LORD, are our Father; our Redeemer
from Everlasting is Your name.*

ISAIAH 63:16

Nothing can take the place of a daily devotional
life with Christ. The great missionary
Hudson Taylor said, "Never mind how great the
pressure is—only where the pressure lies. Never
let it come between you and the Lord, then the
greater pressure, the more it *presses you* to His
heart!" Our quiet time, our prayer time, the time
we spend in the Word is absolutely essential for a
happy Christian life.

—BILLY GRAHAM
The Secret of Happiness

September 28

The Son of Man has come
to seek and to save that which was lost.

LUKE 19:10

God will do what it takes—whatever it takes—to bring his children home.

He is the shepherd in search of His lamb. His legs are scratched, His feet are sore, and His eyes are burning. He scales the cliffs and traverses the fields. He explores the caves. He cups His hands to His mouth and calls into the canyon.

And the name He calls is yours.

—MAX LUCADO
And the Angels were Silent

September 29

Behold, I make all things new.

REVELATION 21:5

I t may not be all that hard to imagine what life in heaven is like. Remember that the best part of getting to heaven is becoming the sorts of persons we were always meant to be, and in our better moments wanted to be, in the loving company of God and all of His children. Once we think of it this way, we can relax while we wait to see with our own eyes what we can only imagine here.

—LEWIS SMEDES
Keeping Hope Alive

September 30

He who has a generous eye will be blessed,
for he gives of his bread to the poor.

PROVERBS 22:9

Remind yourself of God's promises regarding
generosity. God promises if you sow
bountifully, you will reap bountifully. So give!
Give abundantly! Even extravagant giving is
honored by God. I've never known anyone who
went bad because he or she was too generous.
Remind yourself of His promises regarding
generosity and start giving!

—CHARLES R. SWINDOLL
Day by Day

October

*Faith expects from God
what is beyond all expectation.*
ANDREW MURRAY

October 1

*All things work together for good
to those who love God, to those who are the
called according to His purpose.*

ROMANS 8:28

As long as we maintain our dependence on God, He is able to take all the evils that befall us and weave them into His master plan. Our omnipotent God can make even "the wrath of man to praise Him." He can take any sins, any evil, any calamity—no matter where it originated—and make it "work together for good to those who love God."

—CATHERINE MARSHALL
Moments that Matter

*Those who dwell under his shadow
shall return; they shall be revived like grain,
and grow like a vine.*

HOSEA 14:7

God is in the thick of things in your world. He has not taken up residence in a distant galaxy. He has not removed Himself from history. He has not chosen to seclude Himself on a throne in an incandescent castle.

He has drawn near. He has involved Himself in the car pools, heartbreaks, and funeral homes of our day. He is as near to us on Monday as on Sunday. In the school room as in the sanctuary. At the coffee break as much as the communion table.

—MAX LUCADO
And the Angels were Silent

October 3

*Lead me in Your truth and teach me, for You
are the God of my salvation.*

PSALM 25:5

Though change is good, it's rarely easy or
pleasant. We're most interested in pursuing
the comfortable route. We prefer the road more
frequently traveled. Everything within us
scrambles to stay on trails already blazed. But God
often leads us down unknown paths filled with
narrow passages and surprising turns.

—CHARLES R. SWINDOLL
Paul: A Man of Grace and Grit

October 4

*The LORD God is my strength; He will
make my feet like deer's feet, and He will make
me walk on my high hills.*

HABAKKUK 3:19

How do you bring yourself to go on when the roof is caving in on you at the same time as the floor is falling out from under you and the walls are crashing in? Is God even there?

Some situations are so complicated and overwhelming that we're tempted to just walk away and quit. However, we need to explore what God's up to and what He's trying to teach us in the midst of tough times. At pivotal moments like these, we shouldn't push away from God, but run to Him in prayer.

—JOHN HULL AND TIM ELMORE
Pivotal Praying

October 5

If you love Me, keep My commandments.

JOHN 14:15

The cross is not just a symbol of love or a fashion statement. The cross is your daily decision to deny yourself, your rights, your wants, your dreams, your plans, your goals, and deliberately, wholeheartedly, unreservedly live out your commitment to God's will and God's way and God's Word and God's wisdom. The cross is your decision to live for Him. Period.

—ANNE GRAHAM LOTZ
Just Give Me Jesus

October 6

In this is love, not that we loved God,
but that He loved us and sent His son to be the
propitiation for our sins.

1 JOHN 4:10

In the end, all we've ever really wanted is to be loved. "Love comes from God," writes St. John. We don't have to get God to love us by doing something right—even loving Him. "This is love: not that we loved God but that He loved us and sent His Son as an atoning sacrifice for our sins." Someone has noticed, someone has taken initiative. There is nothing we need to do to keep it up, because His love for us is not based on what we've done, but who we are: His beloved.

—BRENT CURTIS AND JOHN ELDREDGE
The Sacred Romance

October 7

*Since we are receiving a kingdom
which cannot be shaken, let us have grace,
by which we may serve God.*

HEBREWS 12:28

God is a God who opens the door and waves His hand, pointing pilgrims to a full table. His invitation is not just for a meal, however. It is for life. An invitation to come into His kingdom and take up residence in a tearless, graveless, painless world. Who can come? Whoever wishes. The invitation is at once universal and personal.

—MAX LUCADO
And the Angels were Silent

October 8

He who loves me will be loved
by My Father, and I will love him.

JOHN 14:21

Jesus purposefully pursued *quiet time* with His
Father—a sacred space worthy of sacrifice,
where the urgent bows to the eternal; a gift—not
a waste—of time for God.

Carving out moments to be alone with God is
an exercise in stillness where we elevate Creator
above creation, "being" above "doing." Where we
listen to the One who is always listening to us.

Resting in God's presence, our soul enjoys a
banquet from God's Word. Our minds forge an
alliance with truth, and dreams are born.

—ALICIA BRITT CHOLE
Pure Joy

*This is the love of God, that we keep
His commandments. And His
commandments are not burdensome.*

1 JOHN 5:3

When we awaken in the morning, we choose the attitude that will ultimately guide our thoughts and actions through the day. I'm convinced our best attitudes emerge out of a clear understanding of our own identity, a clear sense of our divine mission, and a deep sense of God's purpose for our lives. That sort of God-honoring attitude encourages us to press on, to focus on the goal, to respond in remarkable ways to life's most extreme circumstances.

—CHARLES R. SWINDOLL
Paul: A Man of Grace and Grit

October 10

Great peace have those who love Your law,
and nothing causes them to stumble.

PSALM 119:165

Believers who spend time daily in the Word and prayer gradually develop a spiritual radar, a practical wisdom from the Holy Spirit that gives us direction when we need it. Sometimes that direction comes from a promise or warning in Scripture, sometimes from God's providential working in circumstances, and sometimes from the Spirit's witness in our hearts. Even a chance remark by a friend can be used of God to guide us if our minds and hearts are prepared and we're willing to obey God's leading.

— WARREN W. WIERSEBE
The Twenty Essential Qualities

October 11

*His divine power has given to us
all things that pertain to life and godliness, through the
knowledge of Him
who called us by glory and virtue.*

2 PETER 1:3

Many believers do not understand the vast riches they already possess in Jesus Christ, an infinite treasury of wisdom and knowledge and all good things. The moment you accept Him as your Savior you receive everything God is, everything God does, and everything God provides. You lack nothing. God's immeasurable, overflowing love and power are available to you by His grace for every trial, every decision, every challenge.

—CHARLES STANLEY
Into His Presence

October 12

Blessed are the pure in heart,
for they shall see God.

MATTHEW 5:8

Jesus said, "Happy are the pure in heart." Now, we should be able to take that for just what it means. If the heart is the seat of affection, then our love toward God must be pure. If the heart is the center of our motives, then our motives must be pure. If the heart is the residence of our wills, then our wills must be yielded to Christ. We are to be pure in love, pure in motive, and pure in desire.

—BILLY GRAHAM
The Secret of Happiness

October 13

We ought to obey God rather than men.

ACTS 5:29

I f you're getting ready to go off to school or
getting ready to launch a new phase of your
career, don't do it without first establishing a
regular time to meet alone with the Lord. . . .
Your spiritual future depends on it. Without that
commitment to saturate your life with God's Word,
you step into the unknown future at your own risk.

—CHARLES R. SWINDOLL
Paul: A Man of Grace and Grit

October 14

*Those who wait on the LORD shall
renew their strength.*

ISAIAH 40:31

I love that verse. The word *renew* can also be
translated as *exchanged*. In other words, Isaiah
said, "Those who wait on the Lord shall exchange
their strength for His strength." That's a great
exchange, friend! I'd much rather have His
strength than my strength any day, any hour, any
minute, any second!

—LARRY LEA
Wisdom: The Gift Worth Seeking

October 15

*Be steadfast, immovable, always abounding
in the work of the Lord, knowing that your labor
is not in vain in the Lord.*

1 CORINTHIANS 15:58

O ne day, God Himself will take your face in His
hands and gently wipe away your tears as He
reassures you there will be no more suffering.
There will be no more broken homes or broken
hearts, broken lives or broken dreams.

You can look forward with hope, because one
day there will be no more separation, no more
scars, and no more suffering in My Father's House.
It's the home of your dreams!

—ANNE GRAHAM LOTZ
Heaven: My Father's House

October 16

*When my spirit was overwhelmed
within me, then You knew my path.*

PSALM 142:3

Hoping in God is hoping when there is no hope. Hoping in God is to trust that He will be there with us when we put our feet in places so godforsaken that He will be there holding us up when we are falling over the edge. Leading us through our private darkness. Being there—ahead of us, behind us, above us, under us, for us, and even *in* us.

—LEWIS SMEDES
Keeping Hope Alive

October 17

> *"I will be a Father to you, and you shall be*
> *My sons and daughters," says the Lord Almighty.*

2 CORINTHIANS 6:18

God did what we wouldn't dare dream. He did what we couldn't imagine. He became a man so we could trust Him. He became a sacrifice so we could know Him. And He defeated death so we could follow Him.

It defies logic. It is a divine insanity. Holy incredibility.

Only a Creator beyond the fence of logic could offer such a gift of love.

What man can't do, God does.

—MAX LUCADO
And the Angels were Silent

October 18

We are in Him who is true,
in His Son Jesus Christ.

1 JOHN 5:20

We have been shown the way of acceptance on every page of the life of Jesus. It sprang from love and from trust. He set His face like a flint toward Jerusalem. He took up the Cross of His own will. No one could take His life from Him. He deliberately laid it down. He calls us to take up our crosses. That is a different thing from capitulation or resignation. It is a glad and voluntary YES.

—ELISABETH ELLIOT
The Path of Loneliness

October 19

Your righteousness is an everlasting righteousness,
and Your law is truth.

PSALM 119:142

Each of us must become as a little child and by
faith grasp what we cannot altogether
understand. But faith is not a blind leap in the
dark! It is instead based squarely on what God has
done for us in Jesus Christ. Our faith has a firm
foundation, because it is not based on speculation
or wishful thinking, but upon God and His Word.
God can be trusted to keep His promises to us.

—BILLY GRAHAM
The Secret of Happiness

In Your presence is fullness of joy.

PSALM 16:11

David didn't have an easy life either before or after he became king. He was familiar with false accusation, homelessness, failure, betrayal, and family strife. Yet his psalms are filled with expressions of joy.

In spite of circumstances, David chose joy. He could have chosen pity, anger, loneliness, frustration, or fear. He chose joy.

—ALICIA BRITT CHOLE
Pure Joy

October 21

He will speak peace
to His people and to His saints.

PSALM 85:8

I f God says, "I forgive you," who are you to say,
"Thank You, God, but I can't forgive myself"?
Are your standards higher than His? Are you
more righteous than He is? If God says, "I forgive
you," then the only appropriate response is to say,
"God, thank You. I don't deserve it, but I accept it.
And to express my gratitude, I, in turn, forgive that
person who has sinned against me."

—ANNE GRAHAM LOTZ
Just Give Me Jesus

October 22

It is finished!

JOHN 19:30

The dawn of world redemption had broken, and with it the chains of human slavery to sin, shame, and condemnation were being shattered.

"It is finished!" was the Son of God's invitation to join Him in the conviction that now—because of the cross—there is nothing we struggle with that is without either a purpose or an end. No struggle need ever be pointless. No suffering need ever be unending.

—JACK HAYFORD
How to Live Through a Bad Day

October 23

He who is spiritual judges all things,
yet he himself is rightly judged by no one.

1 CORINTHIANS 2:15

God defines the spiritual person as one who judges all things. This means that the truly spiritual person is capable of discerning between natural wisdom and spiritual wisdom. The truly spiritual person is able to discern what God is truly saying about a matter and then acts on it.

Our challenge is to . . . decide it is God's answers and God's solutions that we truly want in our lives.

—LARRY LEA
Wisdom: The Gift Worth Seeking

October 24

*The LORD is near to those
who have a broken heart, and saves such
as have a contrite spirit.*

PSALM 34:18

In brokenness and contrition the humbled person cries out to God for help. He reaches out to Christ for restoration and healing. He exercises faith in another because he knows he must touch someone greater than himself. Similarly he seeks out others he can serve and in his suffering service finds fulfillment and freedom from himself.

It is to such souls that God gives Himself gladly, freely.

—PHILLIP KELLER
A Gardner Looks at the Fruits of the Spirit

October 25

As the heavens are high above the earth,
so great is His mercy toward those who fear Him.

PSALM 103:11

Adversity can be handled one of two ways.
Either you can deal with it on your own, or you
can allow God to carry your burden for you. The first
requires human strength and effort, which are rarely
sufficient in handling grievous trials. Heartache
erodes human ability.

The wiser course of action is to allow God to
handle your adversity. His ability to provide goes
beyond our greatest imagination. He is the God who
has the ability to calm every storm.

—CHARLES STANLEY
Into His Presence

October 26

*We have a building from God, a house
not made with hands, eternal in the heavens.*

2 CORINTHIANS 5:5

Earth's heartaches are healed by the promises
of God. When we are home at last, the
homesickness will be over. We shall praise the King
who knew how to cut eternal doorways in mere
holes cut in sod. Joy belongs to all those who
understand that earth is but a rehearsal for heaven.

On dim evenings, if you squint at sunsets, you
can all but see the promise. In our Father's house
there really are many mansions—and one of them
is ours.

—CALVIN MILLER
Into the Depths of God

*The person who continues
to be strong until the end will be saved.*

MATTHEW 24:13, NCV

The Brazilians have a great phrase for this. In Portuguese, a person who has the ability to hang in and not give up has *garra*. *Garra* means "claws." What imagery! A person with *garra* has claws which burrow in the side of the cliff and keep him from falling.

So do the saved. They may get close to the edge, they may even stumble and slide. But they will dig their nails into the rock of God and hang on.

—MAX LUCADO
And the Angels were Silent

October 28

Delight yourself also in the LORD, and
He shall give you the desires of your heart.

PSALM 37:4

This promise is not carte blanche to get what we want from God just because we belong to His family. David is saying that, if we truly delight in the Lord, we will want to know Him better; and the better we know Him, the more we will become like Him. *His* desires will become *our* desires, and our greatest desires will be to know Him even more and enjoy Him in an ever-deepening way.

—WARREN W. WIERSEBE
The Twenty Essential Qualities

October 29

*Commit your way to the LORD, trust
also in Him, and He shall bring it to pass.*

PSALM 37:5

Acceptance of discipleship is the utter
abandonment of the disciple, the surrender of
all rights, to the Master. This abandonment, in all
cases, will mean pain. Christ listed some of the
troubles His followers could expect, so they would
not be taken by surprise and thus discard their
faith in Him. He did not offer immunity. He asked
for trust.

—ELISABETH ELLIOT
The Path of Loneliness

October 30

*The fear of the LORD leads to life,
and he who has it will abide in satisfaction.*

PROVERBS 19:23

S ometimes the wisdom of God will be a bitter
herb to you. It will be contrary to the way you
want to do things or the way you want to
experience life. But if you will swallow that bitter
pill—or, in other words, go ahead and DO what
you know to do, no matter how hard it is and no
matter how much you have to ENDURE—then
you'll find yourself in a position to be resurrected
by God with great victory!

—LARRY LEA
Wisdom: The Gift Worth Seeking

October 31

Trust in the LORD and do good.

PSALM 37:3

If you wish to be a man or woman of God who desires to live a godly life that will leave its mark upon this world, you must stand in the shadow of your Savior. Trust Him to work through the trials you encounter, through the extreme circumstances you cannot handle on your own. He is still the God of impossible situations. He does what no earthly individual can do.

—CHARLES R. SWINDOLL
Day by Day

November

*God is never away off
somewhere else, He is always there.*

OSWALD CHAMBERS

November 1

As for God, His way is perfect.

PSALM 18:30

I s anyone perfect? No, not anyone on earth. Only God is perfect! And you don't need to be God—not in your own appraisal of yourself or in relation to anybody. You are free to simply be you.

There will always be aspects of you that fall short of some idealized goal. As you are able to recognize and accept these aspects, you will have a chance to modify them and improve them. And you will set other people free to do the same.

—NEIL CLARK WARREN
God Said It, Don't Sweat It

Greater love has no one than this,
than to lay down one's life for his friends.

JOHN 15:13

The only crown Jesus ever wore on earth was a crown of thorns.

What does that crown tell us about the love of God the Father? Much every way. For one thing, it tells us that His love is not a sentimental thing, for it was strong enough to hurt His own Son. He could have rescued Him with "legions of angels." He did not do so.

What does the crown of thorns tell us about the love of God the Son? It tells us that it was strong enough to deny itself, strong enough to suffer.

—ELISABETH ELLIOT
The Path of Loneliness

November 3

The Lord himself will come down
from heaven, with a loud command.

1 THESSALONIANS 4:16, NIV

Have you ever wondered what that command will be? It will be the inaugural word of heaven.

I could very well be wrong, but I think the command that puts an end to the pains of the earth and initiates the joys of heaven will be two words: "No more."

No more loneliness. No more tears. No more death. No more sadness. No more crying. No more pain.

—MAX LUCADO
And the Angels were Silent

November 4

You have always been, and
You will always be. To You, a thousand
years is like the passing of a day.

PSALM 90:2, 4, NCV

God is intimately involved in every nanosecond of every moment of every day in every life. Even when the time of your life seems totally out of control, speeding and changing so that you can barely catch your breath, He is behind every tick of the clock. And when life slows down to a crawl through boredom or depression, He still holds you firm in His sight.

—PETER WALLACE
What the Psalmist Is Saying to You

November 5

*I delight to do Your will, O my God, and
Your law is within my heart.*

PSALM 40:8

The situation that looms in front of you may seem impossible to overcome in your own strength. It might be the result of your own actions, or you may be an innocent victim, caught in the backlash of someone else's consequences. Whatever the case, we can easily become intimidated, even fearful, and eventually immobile. The only way to move beyond that sort of paralyzing stalemate is to learn to accept and trust God's plan. You release the controls and wait for Him to move.

—CHARLES R. SWINDOLL
Paul: A Man of Grace and Grit

November 6

*Truly our fellowship is with the Father and
with His Son Jesus Christ.*

1 JOHN 1:3

Jesus had a humble heart. If He abides in us,
pride will never dominate our lives. Jesus had a
loving heart. If He dwells within us, hatred and
bitterness will never rule us. Jesus had a forgiving
and understanding heart. If He lives within us,
mercy will temper our relationships with our
fellowmen.

—BILLY GRAHAM,
The Secret of Happiness

*I do not seek My own will but the will
of the Father who sent Me.*

JOHN 5:30

Wherever Christ moved, whomever He met, whatever circumstances He encountered, the remarkable aspect of His life was that He was always in control. He was never taken unawares, never caught in a crisis. Jesus was never manipulated, nor was He ever at the mercy of the mob.

Jesus of Nazareth, the Christ of God, was supremely in control. And this was because He was God-controlled.

—PHILLIP KELLER
A Gardner Looks at the Fruits of the Spirit

November 8

Though He was rich, yet for your sakes
He became poor, that you through His poverty might
become rich.

2 CORINTHIANS 8:9

During His earthly ministry, Jesus not only shared precious gifts with needy people—sight to the blind, food to the hungry, healing to the sick, even life to the dead—but Jesus gave Himself for all people so that anybody who trusted Him would share the riches of His grace. Furthermore, He didn't simply take away the bad and replace it with the good, Jesus took on Himself all that was bad in us, including our sins, so that He might share with us all the good that is in Him.

—WARREN W. WIERSEBE
The Twenty Essential Qualities

November 9

Now abide faith, hope, love, these three;
but the greatest of these is love.

1 CORINTHIANS 13:13

Paul not only distinguishes among faith, hope, and love, but also links them to show that they remain connected and mutually dependent on each other. The biblical concept of hope does not lack the confidence that our cultural concept of hope does.

Rather, hope is faith looking forward to the future. It is a hope that will not disappoint or leave us ashamed.

—R. C. SPROUL
Loved By God

The LORD will perfect that which
concerns me; Your mercy, O LORD, endures forever.

PSALM 138:8

To magnify something, you make it look larger, increasing it out of proportion. To talk about ourselves or our activities out of true proportion is dangerous indeed, but when we magnify God, we are on safe ground. We simply cannot say too much about God's goodness or love. The most exaggerated things we can think of will still be far below what is actually the case.

—RICHARD FOSTER
Prayer: Finding the Heart's True Home

November 11

*Count it all joy when you fall
into various trials, knowing that the testing
of your faith produces patience.*

JAMES 1:2

Trials, James tells us, prove the authenticity of
our faith.

Truth is, we would rather be perfected and
completed by viewing a motivational video,
attending a challenging conference, reading an
inspiring book (about someone else who went
through trials), or . . . anything but testing! . . .

We long for controlled, comfortable,
circumstances. But pure joy is the fruit of tested,
patient, faith.

—ALICIA BRITT CHOLE
Pure Joy

November 12

> *My God shall supply all your need according*
> *to His riches in glory by Christ Jesus.*
>
> PHILIPPIANS 4:19

God is in control. When a job is terminated, a mate quits, a friend deserts, God is quietly but sovereignly at work for your good. You are not a victim of the economy or another's decision.

You can be content in any circumstance when you are sure of God's unceasing care and absolute control over every detail. Rest in His ability, and contentment will follow.

—CHARLES STANLEY
Into His Presence

November 13

*Come to Me, all you who labor and
are heavy laden, and I will give you rest.*

MATTHEW 11:28

God is an inviting God. He invited Mary to
birth His Son, the disciples to fish for men,
the adulteress woman to start over, and Thomas to
touch His wounds. God is the King who prepares
the palace, sets the table, and invites His subjects
to come in.

God is a God who invites. God is a God who calls.

—MAX LUCADO
And the Angels Were Silent

November 14

In My Father's house are many mansions.

JOHN 14:2

Heaven is a big place! "In my Father's house are many mansions"—room enough for anyone and everyone who chooses to be a member of God's family! So please feel free to invite your entire family—including in-laws and out-laws, every one of your friends, all of your neighbors, the total population of your city, your state, your nation— everybody in the whole wide world!

—ANNE GRAHAM LOTZ
Heaven: My Father's House

He who follows righteousness and
mercy finds life, righteousness and honor.

PROVERBS 21:21

Wisdom isn't for heaven. It's for NOW, on this
earth.

Wisdom isn't just for the knowing. It's for the
doing.

Wisdom isn't for your mind. It's for your
hands and feet to implement.

God imparts wisdom to you so you can make a
difference in this world . . . so you can extend His
kingdom . . . so you can enter into the fullness of
His blessings for you.

—LARRY LEA
Wisdom: The Gift Worth Seeking

*I bow my knees to the Father of our
Lord Jesus Christ, from whom the whole family
in heaven and earth is named.*

EPHESIANS 3:14–15

Y ou've seen people treat this world like it was a permanent home. It's not. You've seen people pour time and energy into life like it will last forever. It won't. You've seen people so proud of what they have done, that they hope they will never have to leave—they will.

We all will. We are in transit. Someday the plane will stop and the deboarding will begin. Wise are those who are ready when the pilot says to get off.

—MAX LUCADO
And the Angels were Silent

November 17

*Love your enemies,
do good, . . . and your reward will be great.*

LUKE 6:35

We may be tempted sometimes to conclude that because God doesn't fix our problem He doesn't love us. There are many things that He does not fix precisely *because He loves us.* Instead of extracting us from the problem, He calls us. In our sorrow or loneliness or pain He calls—"This is a necessary part of the journey. Even if it is the roughest part, it is only a part, and it will not last the whole long way. Remember where I am leading you. Remember what you will find at the end—a home and a haven and a heaven."

—ELISABETH ELLIOT
The Path of Loneliness

November 18

*Let your light so shine before men,
that they may see your good works and glorify
your Father in heaven.*

MATTHEW 5:16

To the watching world, our lives paint a portrait
of God. Our responses to times of gladness and
sorrow are like paintbrushes sweeping across the
canvass of life, leaving impressions of the God we
call Savior. Through our actions and attitudes
seekers gather information about this Jesus we
proclaim.

With the help of the Holy Spirit, may our lives
paint a picture of our God who is . . . patient but not
passive . . . accepting but not pliable . . . holy but
not untouchable . . . near but not us.

—ALICIA BRITT CHOLE
Pure Joy

He will not allow your foot to be moved;
He who keeps you will not slumber.

PSALM 121:3

The Lord is a personal God, not limited by time or space, One who inhabits the hearts of all who believe in Him. Therefore, no temple or building can contain His presence because He is eternally present throughout the universe.

Have you ever thought that God is with you in all you do and say throughout the day? He is not just present in the morning when you awake. He is with you in the grocery store, in the doctor's office, at work, even at play. No matter where you go, God goes with you.

—CHARLES STANLEY
Into His Presence

November 20

> *Be ready, for the Son of Man is*
> *coming at an hour you do not expect.*

MATTHEW 24:44

Every person who has ever lived will be present at that final gathering. Every heart that has ever beat. Every mouth that has ever spoken. On that day you will be surrounded by a sea of people. Rich, poor. Famous, unknown. Kings, bums. Brilliant, demented. All will be present. And all will be looking in one direction. All will be looking at Him—the Son of Man. Wrapped in splendor. Shot through with radiance.

—MAX LUCADO
And the Angels were Silent

November 21

It is God who works in you both
to will and to do for His good pleasure.

PHILIPPIANS 2:13

It is utterly absurd to assume or suppose that a person who is determined to do his own will can ever please God. Only as our wills are brought into harmony and submission to His will do we discover the secret of divine power and productivity.

One short sentence sums up this whole subject: "Not my will, but Thine be done."

—PHILLIP KELLER
A Gardner Looks at the Fruits of the Spirit

November 22

*Blessed is the man [whose] delight is
in the law of the LORD.*

PSALM 1:1-2

To delight in God's truth means we take time
daily to read the Word and meditate on it,
and to rejoice when He speaks to us from the
sacred page, teaching us a new truth or giving us
a new application of a familiar truth.

But the important thing is that we see God
and hear His voice as we read His Word. It isn't
enough merely to know the truth of God in a
doctrinal way; we must also know the God of truth
in a personal way.

—WARREN W. WIERSEBE
The Twenty Essential Qualities

November 23

*Through wisdom a house is
built, . . . by knowledge the rooms are filled.*

PROVERBS 24:3–4

You may be one who lives your life pursuing
fame and fortune, depending on the applause
of others. Bad plan. To begin with, fortune has
shallow rules. The winds of adversity can quickly
blow it all away. Fame is as fickle as the last
response from the crowd. Learn a dual lesson.

When you're praised and applauded, don't pay
any attention. When you're rejected and abused,
don't quit.

—CHARLES R. SWINDOLL
Paul: A Man of Grace and Grit

November 24

You were not redeemed with
corruptible things, like silver or gold ... but
with the precious blood of Christ.

1 PETER 1:18-19

We are free either to love God or not. He invites us to love Him. He urges us to love Him. He came that we might love Him. But, in the end, the choice is yours and mine. To take that choice from each of us, for Him to force us to love Him, would be less than love.

God explains the benefits, outlines the promises, and articulates very clearly the consequences. And then, in the end, He leaves the choice to us.

—MAX LUCADO
And the Angels were Silent

November 25

We, according to His promise,
look for new heavens and a new earth in
which righteousness dwells.

2 PETER 3:13

If God could make the heavens and earth as beautiful as we think they are today—which includes thousands of years of wear and tear, corruption and pollution, sin and selfishness—can you imagine what the new Heaven and the new earth will look like?

—ANNE GRAHAM LOTZ
Heaven: My Father's House

November 26

*How precious also are Your thoughts
to me, O God! How great is the sum of them!*

PSALM 139:17

When I itch for heaven I find that what I really want there is the fulfillment of all that is good about life now—but with its beauty never blotched with ugliness, its pleasure never choked by pain, its plenty never mocked by unfairness to others, its truth never hid by falsehood, its goodness never compromised by evil—and the discovery every day anew that our very beings are alive with God. In short, total fulfillment. Which is, I suppose, what we want when we want heaven.

—LEWIS SMEDES
Keeping Hope Alive

November 27

> *You are my hiding place*
> *and my shield; I hope in Your word.*

PSALM 119:114

I firmly believe God's Word has been preserved, not merely as a collection of historical documents and geographical studies, but as a trustworthy resource—a place we turn to for assistance in living our lives in ways that honor Christ.

In the pages of Scripture, God has given us models—people, believe it or not, who are just like you and me, who, despite the odds, lived lives pleasing to Him. By faith. In obedience. With courage.

—CHARLES R. SWINDOLL
Paul: A Man of Grace and Grit

November 28

Light is sown for the righteous,
and gladness for the upright in heart.

PSALM 97:11

God's light pours down over us, even in the darkness. It illuminates the thoughts of our minds, the emotions of the heart. It brightens our pathway.

God sows the light of His Word in our souls as a farmer sows seeds in the ground. The seeds take root, send out tender shoots, grow strong and green and fresh, and ultimately provide fruit.

—PETER WALLACE
What the Psalmist Is Saying to You

November 29

*Behold, this is our God; we have
waited for Him, and He will save us.*

ISAIAH 25:9

When people don't listen, remember Jesus.
When tears come, remember Jesus. When
disappointment is your bed partner, remember
Jesus. When fear pitches his tent in your front
yard. When death looms, when anger simmers,
when shame weighs heavily. Remember Jesus.

Remember the dead called from the grave with
a Galilean accent. Remember the eyes of God that
wept human tears.

—MAX LUCADO
Six Hours, One Day

November 30

You wove me in my mother's womb.
I will give thanks to You, for I am fearfully
and wonderfully made.

PSALM 139:13-14, NASB

God reached into my life when I was merely a tiny embryo and began to shape me within. He originated me. He began to put me together while I was still in the soft silence of my mother's womb. . . .

Mother Nature didn't make me. Fate did not shape me, neither was I just a biological combination of mother and dad in a moment of sexual passion. Nor was I conceived through blind chance. You, God (and no other), made me!

—CHARLES R. SWINDOLL
Day by Day

December

God's love is a sun that never sets.

ARTHUR JOHN GOSSIP

December 1

> *If they could be made God's*
> *people by what they did, then God's gift*
> *of grace would not really be a gift.*

ROMANS 11:6, NCV

To whom does God offer His gift? To the brightest? The most beautiful or the most charming? No. His gift is for us all—beggars and bankers, clergy and clerks, judges and janitors. All God's children.

And He wants us so badly, He'll take us in any condition—"as is" reads the tag on our collars. . . .

He wants us *now*.

—MAX LUCADO
No Wonder They Call Him the Savior

December 2

He who overcomes shall inherit all things,
and I will be his God and he shall be My son.

REVELATION 21:7

What shall it be like in heaven?

Some of our truest images of ourselves in heaven, it seems to me, are stirred up by bread-and-butter pleasures we enjoy here. Have a thigh-thumping laugh at a ridiculous story, and you get a sharp snap of yourself happy in heaven. Let a piece of soul music send shivers down your spine, and you have an image of your capacity for beauty in heaven.... Maybe the happiest memories of ourselves on earth are our clearest images of what we shall be in heaven.

—LEWIS SMEDES
Keeping Hope Alive

December 3

The mercy of the LORD is from
everlasting to everlasting on those who fear Him.

PSALM 103:17

Those who saw Jesus—really saw Him—knew
there was something different. At His touch
blind beggars saw. At His command crippled legs
walked. At His embrace empty lives filled with vision.

He fed thousands with one basket. He stilled a
storm with one command. He raised the dead with
one proclamation. He changed lives with one
request. He rerouted the history of the world with
one life, lived in one country, was born in one
manger, and died on one hill.

—MAX LUCADO
And the Angels were Silent

*But the LORD is the true God; He is
the living God and the everlasting King.*

JEREMIAH 10:10

Looking down over the battlements of heaven
God saw this planet swinging in space—
doomed, damned, crushed, and bound for hell.
He saw you and me struggling beneath our load
of sin. He made His decision.

The angelic hosts bowed in humility and awe
as heaven's Lord of Lords, who could speak worlds
into space, got into His jeweled chariot, went back
through pearly gates, across the steep of the skies,
and on a black Judean night, while the stars sang
together and the escorting angels chanted His
praise, stepped out of the chariot, threw off His
robes, and became man!

—BILLY GRAHAM
Peace with God

December 5

*Where your treasure is,
there your heart will be also.*

MATTHEW 6:21

The physical body you live in. The family you were born into. The opportunities that have crossed your path. The faith you have. All are ultimately from God. Even the breath you breathe every minute is a gift from God. . . .

God has given you these gifts to see what you will do with them. He is watching to see if you are greedy. He is watching to see if you are going to trust money more than you trust Him.

—LARRY LEA
Wisdom: The Gift Worth Seeking

December 6

*This hope we have as an anchor
of the soul, a hope both sure and steadfast.*

HEBREWS 6:19, NASB

God keeps His promises. It's a major part of His immutable nature. He doesn't hold out hope with nice-sounding words, then renege on what He said He would do. God is neither fickle nor moody. And He never lies. As my own father used to say of people with integrity. "His word is His bond."

—CHARLES R. SWINDOLL
Elijah

He lays the beams of His upper chambers
in the waters, Who makes the clouds
His chariot, Who walks on the wings of the
wind, Who makes His angels spirits.

PSALM 104:3-4

God establishes the rain that waters and
nourishes the earth in the clouds of the sky.

He moves around and above us on a chariot of
clouds, "on the wings of the wind."

He summons and sends out His angelic
ministers to work His will in the earth—protecting,
guiding, providing.

He is working continually, establishing His
will, answering prayers, touching lives, healing sick
hearts. Even in your life.

—PETER WALLACE
What the Psalmist Is Saying to You

December 8

*Come to me, all you who labor and
are heavy laden, and I will give you rest.*

MATTHEW 11:28

Most of us think of spiritual progress as requiring us to do more, even as our heart cries out to us to lay our burdens down. We renew our efforts at Bible study, Scripture memory, and Christian service, fearing that we will be discovered in our weakness and need. We try to use whatever small story we have been living in—competence, gifted speaking, service to others, and so on—to cross the chasm between living in the flesh and living spiritually, when only Christ can carry us to rest.

—BRENT CURTIS AND JOHN ELDREDGE
The Sacred Romance

December 9

*One thing I have desired of the LORD, . . . that I may
dwell in the house of the LORD all the days of my life,
to behold the beauty of the LORD.*

PSALM 27:4

The beauty of God describes His moral
character. God is holy, pure, just, loving, wise,
longsuffering, merciful, gracious, and so much
more; and these attributes exist in perfect
harmony and are manifested in perfectly balanced
ways. God's beauty is the beauty of perfection, a
beauty that borrows from nothing and no one and
to which nothing or no one may be compared.

—WARREN W. WIERSEBE
The Twenty Essential Qualities

December 10

*God so loved the world that He gave His
only begotten Son, that whoever believes in Him should
not perish but have everlasting life.*

JOHN 3:16

An ordinary night with ordinary sheep and ordinary shepherds. And were it not for a God who loves to hook an "extra" on the front of the ordinary, the night would have gone unnoticed. The sheep would have been forgotten, and the shepherds would have slept the night away.

But God dances amidst the common. And that night He did a waltz....

The night was ordinary no more.

—MAX LUCADO
The Applause of Heaven

December 11

No eye has seen, no ear has heard,
no mind has conceived what God has prepared
for those who love him.

1 CORINTHIANS 2:9, NIV

P aul simply means we cannot outdream God.
What is at the end of our personal journeys?
Something beyond our wildest imagination.

—BRENT CURTIS AND JOHN ELDREDGE
The Sacred Romance

December 12

God is a safe place to hide,
ready to help when we need him.

PSALM 46:1, *THE MESSAGE*

Have you ever asked God for something that He did not give you? At first, you might have felt slighted or upset, but perhaps much later you saw the reason why God said no.

God promises to give only what is good for you and no less. Why? The Lord loves you with an affection beyond imagination, and He fashioned every intricate fiber of your being. It makes sense, then, that He knows exactly what you need and what blessings would benefit you.

—CHARLES STANLEY
Into His Presence

December 13

He was wounded for our transgressions,
He was bruised for our iniquities.

ISAIAH 53:5

There is no way our little minds can comprehend the love of God. But that didn't keep Him from coming. . . .

From the cradle in Bethlehem to the cross in Jerusalem we've pondered the love of our Father. What can you say to that kind of emotion? Upon learning that God would rather die than live without you, how do you react? How can you begin to explain such passion?

—MAX LUCADO
In the Grip of Grace

*Those who are wise shall shine
like the brightness of the firmament.*

DANIEL 12:3

I am amazed to see, how frequently the giving of
gifts is mentioned in the Bible. . . . Rebekah
accepts gifts of jewelry and clothing, symbolic of
her acceptance if Isaac as her husband. Jacob tries
to give a lavish present of livestock to the brother
he has wronged. . . . Wise Men bring gifts to an
Infant—gold, which acknowledges their King,
frankincense their God, myrrh their Redeemer.

—CATHERINE MARSHALL
Moments that Matter

December 15

*The sufferings of this present time
are not worthy to be compared with the glory
which shall be revealed in us.*

ROMANS 8:18

A s humans we tend to focus on the immediate.
Yet all the while, God is orchestrating the
entirety of our lives, using specific details, specific
people, specific circumstances, specific words.
We tend to look at one piece of the puzzle, while
God sees the whole picture as well as the detailed
specifics within each piece. We see things in black
and white, while God sees things in panoramic color.

—JOHN HULL AND TIM ELMORE
Pivotal Praying

December 16

If anyone serves Me, let him follow Me.

JOHN 12:26

God deals differently with each of us. He knows no "typical" case. He seeks us out at a point in our own need and longing and runs down the road to meet us. This individualized treatment should delight rather than confuse us, because it so clearly reveals the highly personal quality of God's love and concern.

—CATHERINE MARSHALL
Moments that Matter

*Present your bodies a living
sacrifice, holy, acceptable to God, which is
your reasonable service.*

ROMANS 12:1

L ife is full of journeys. Some are dull excursions
we grudgingly take out of sheer duty. Others
are thrilling adventures we embark on with eyes
of faith. But changes await you . . . changes in you.

No journey is more life changing than your
inner spiritual journey back to the Cross. In all
your travels, have you gone there? If not, are you
willing to take that first step? It's a journey you will
never regret. I can assure you, and one you
will never forget.

—CHARLES R. SWINDOLL
Paul: A Man of Grace and Grit

December 18

Those who sow in tears shall reap in joy.

PSALM 126:5

God does not waste our tears. He counts and invests each one. Tears of brokenness water the dry and parched places in our souls and in our world.

One more ingredient is essential though if our tears are to produce fruit: *sowing.*

In the midst of pain, we are to give. In the midst of heartache, we are to serve.

Brokenness – service = bitterness
Brokenness + service = fruitfulness

—ALICIA BRITT CHOLE
Pure Joy

December 19

*The Son of Man will come in the glory
of His Father with His angels, and then He will
reward each according to his works.*

MATTHEW 16:27

I f with courage and joy we pour ourselves out for
God and for others for His sake, it is not possible
to lose, in any final sense, anything worth keeping.
We will lose ourselves and our selfishness.
We will gain everything worth having.

—ELISABETH ELLIOT
The Path of Loneliness

December 20

For the grace of God that
brings salvation has appeared to all men.

TITUS 2:11

As moments go, that one appeared no different than any others. . . . It came and went. . . . It was one of the countless moments that have marked time since eternity became measurable.

But in reality, that particular moment was like none other. For through that segment of time a spectacular thing occurred. God became a man. While the creatures of earth walked unaware, Divinity arrived.

—MAX LUCADO
God Came Near

As a father pities his children,
so the LORD pities those who fear Him.

PSALM 103:13

A re you feeling crushed and confused,
misunderstood and beaten down? Resist the
temptation to roll up your sleeves and muster a self-
imposed recovery plan. This is your opportunity!
Rather than fighting back, surrender. Embrace your
weakness. Tell your heavenly Father you are trusting
in the strength of His power. *Look up!*

—CHARLES R. SWINDOLL
Paul: A Man of Grace and Grit

December 22

Happy are the people whose
God is the LORD!

PSALM 144:15

We are God's treasure! When God the Father
looked throughout the universe for
something to give His only Son in reward for what
He had accomplished on earth, the Father
handpicked you! You are the Father's priceless gift
of love to the Son!

—ANNE GRAHAM LOTZ
Heaven: My Father's House

*Therefore by their
fruits you will know them.*

MATTHEW 7:20

Fruit production in our Christian experience,
just as in an orchard or garden, is not
something that goes on with great fanfare, noise or
theatrics. From the opening of the first tiny bud
under the impulse of spring sunshine, to the
perfect ripening of the fully formed fruit beneath
late Indian summer skies, the whole process goes
on quietly, serenely, and surely. It is the Spirit of
God who by His presence within guarantees
growth, maturity, and conformity to Christ.

—PHILLIP KELLER
A Gardner Looks at the Fruits of the Spirit

December 24

I will meditate on the glorious splendor
of Your majesty, and on Your wondrous works.

PSALM 145:5

Has it been a while since you stared at the
heavens is speechless amazement? Has it
been awhile since you realized God's divinity and
your carnality?

If it has, then you need to know something. He is
still there. He hasn't left. Under all those papers and
books and reports and years. In the midst of all those
voices and faces and memories and pictures, He is
still there.

Do yourself a favor. Stand before Him again.

—MAX LUCADO
Six Hours, One Day

December 25

*They shall obtain joy and gladness and
sorrow and sighing shall flee away.*

ISAIAH 35:10

The black, velvety sky was clear and studded
with sparkling stars that had looked down on
Earth since the beginning of time. On the clear
night air, sound traveled easily and somewhere
from the direction of the village inn someone
slammed a door.

The Seed of the woman, Who would open
heaven's gate and welcome any and all who place
their faith in Him . . . had been given!

The Hope that was born that night continues
to radiate down through the years until it envelops
your heart and mine.

—ANNE GRAHAM LOTZ
God's Story

December 26

*Peace I leave with you, My peace I give to you;
not as the world gives do I give to you.*

JOHN 14:27

Jesus didn't leave a material inheritance to His disciples. All He had when He died was a robe, which went to the Roman soldiers; His mother, whom He turned over to His brother John; His body, which He gave to Joseph of Arimathea; and His Spirit, which returned to His Father.

But Jesus willed His followers something more valuable than gold, more enduring than vast landholdings and more to be desired than palaces of marble—He willed us His peace.

—BILLY GRAHAM
The Secret of Happiness

December 27

The street of the city was pure gold,
like transparent glass.

REVELATION 21:21

The Bible tells us that when we get to Heaven all of our sins and flaws will fall away, and we will be like Jesus. With our unique personalities and characteristics, every single one of us is going to perfectly reflect the character of Christ. And as we walk on streets that reflect like mirrors, every step we take and every move we make is going to bring glory to Him.

—ANNE GRAHAM LOTZ
Heaven: My Father's House

December 28

He who believes in Me, as the Scripture
has said, out of his heart
will flow rivers of living water.

JOHN 7:38

Remember the words of Jesus to the Samaritan woman? "The water I give will become a spring of water gushing up inside that person, giving eternal life" (John 4:14, NCV). Jesus offers, not a singular drink of water, but a perpetual artesian well! And the well isn't a hole in your backyard but the Holy Spirit of God in your heart.

—MAX LUCADO
He Chose the Nails

December 29

I am with you always,
even to the end of the age.

MATTHEW 28:20

Remember, Christ is always near us. We should say nothing that we would not wish to say in His Presence. We should do nothing that we would not do in His Presence. We should go no place that we would not go in His Presence. But He is not with us just to judge or condemn us; He is near to comfort, protect, guide, encourage, strengthen, and help.

—BILLY GRAHAM
The Secret of Happiness

December 30

He who receives Me
receives Him who sent Me.

MATTHEW 10:40

How do you simplify faith? How do you get rid of the clutter? How do you discover a joy worth waking up to?

Simplify your faith by seeking God for yourself. No confusing ceremonies necessary. No mysterious rituals required. No elaborate channels of command or levels of access.

You have a Bible? You can study. You have a heart? You can pray. You have a mind. You can think.

— MAX LUCADO
And the Angels were Silent

December 31

The way of the LORD is a stronghold to the upright.... The righteous will never be shaken.

PROVERBS 10:29–30, NASB

Webster defines hope, "to desire with expectation of fulfillment." To hope is to anticipate. It is more than dreaming, however. It is possessing within ourselves an expectation that someday there will be the fulfillment of that desire. It will become a reality. Hope always looks to the future, it's always on tiptoes. It keeps us going. It makes a dismal today bearable because it promises a brighter tomorrow.

—CHARLES R. SWINDOLL
Dropping Your Guard

Acknowledgments

Grateful acknowledgment is made to the following publishers for permission to reprint this copyrighted material.

Burroughs, Esther. *Splash the Living Water* (Nashville: Thomas Nelson, 1999).

Chole, Alicia Britt. *Pure Joy* (Nashville: J. Countryman, 2003).

Curtis, Brent and John Eldredge. *The Sacred Romance* (Nashville: Thomas Nelson, 1997).

Elliot, Elisabeth. *The Path of Loneliness* (Nashville: Thomas Nelson, 1988).

——*Keep a Quiet Heart* (Ann Arbor: Servant Publications, 1995).

Eldredge, John. *The Journey of Desire* (Nashville: Thomas Nelson, 2000).

Foster, Richard. *Prayer: Finding the Hearts True Home* (New York: HarperCollins, 1992).

Graham, Billy. *Peace with God* (Nashville: W Publishing Group, 1984).

——*The Secret of Happiness* (Nashville: W Publishing Group, 2002).

Hayford, Jack. *How to Live Through a Bad Day* (Nashville: Thomas Nelson, 2001).

Hull, John and Tim Elmore. *Pivotal Praying* (Nashville, Thomas Nelson, 2002).